STOP WORRYING,
HE REIGNS

Stop Worrying, He Reigns

A Study of the Puzzle Pieces of the Book of Esther

JUSTIN MILLER

WIPF & STOCK · Eugene, Oregon

Wipf & Stock
An Imprint of Wipf and Stock Publishers
199 W. 8th Ave., Suite 3
Eugene, OR 97401

www.wipfandstock.com

PAPERBACK ISBN: 978-1-5326-7023-7
HARDCOVER ISBN: 978-1-5326-7024-4
EBOOK ISBN: 978-1-5326-7025-1

Manufactured in the U.S.A.   NOVEMBER 19, 2018

To JoDawn, my bride and best friend. God's kindness knows no bounds. He saved me and gave me you to sojourn in this world with. His grace truly is amazing.

Contents

Introduction

IF GOD IS GOOD, then he cannot be all powerful, and if God is all powerful, he cannot be good. I remember hearing this statement and being perplexed with the issue it brought forth. To some degree or another, we all have seen great distress, hurt, suffering, and pain in the world we live in. Evil is a concept every human innately knows. How does a good God sovereignly rule over and in a fallen world? Why, if God is good, does a fallen world exist? These questions find their answers in the truths that emerge from a study of the book of Esther. A book that never mentions God's name or acknowledges him in the story, is ultimately a book that is all about him. The truth of Scripture is that God is good and God is all-powerful. Those two realities are not in tension with one another, but rather are perfectly expressed through God's providential sovereignty over all his creation. Evil exists because mankind exists. God does all things for his glory, and only in a fallen world will you see God's grace, justice, unconditional love, mercy, righteousness, etc., come forth. God, in his power, accomplishes his good ends with his creation by providentially guiding fallen humanity. God is good. God is all powerful. As you study the book of Esther, my hope is that those realities are pressed deeply into your conscience and stir your affections for a God who is altogether infinitely marvelous to behold. His goodness is seen in the pages of Esther. His reign and power over all things are glaringly evident as the story progresses. God reigns over kingdoms and kings. He reigns over storms and still waters. He reigns over all creation, and he is good.

The reality of God's reign over history is the remedy for the anxiety many of his people experience in a rapidly changing world. The reality of God's sovereignty and providence is the cure for much of the fear and anxiety that hinders the church and its mission to magnify the Lord Jesus Christ amongst all peoples. From the narrative of Esther, we are called to stop worrying, for God reigns.

1

The Mess of Puzzle Pieces
(Esther 1–2)

THE SKY IS FALLING! The sky is falling! One of my children's favorite movies is "Chicken Little." They love how it opens with this little teenage chicken ringing the warning bell of the town he loves and lives in while at the same time, with great angst and urgency, proclaiming to all who hear him that "The sky is falling!" Ironically enough, many in the evangelical church are ringing that same warning bell, while yelling to all who will listen, "the sky is falling, the sky is falling!" They seem to believe that the recent moral trends and political movements in our country spell almost certain doom for the church. However, is the sky really falling for the evangelical church? Should we be anxious and fearful about the future of our Western world and its relationship to Biblical Christianity? A young man into whom I spent a lot of time investing the Word would always tell me that Christianity would perish in the Western world if it did not embrace certain secular or scientific beliefs. He spoke of Christianity's need to acknowledge macroevolution, homosexuality, etc., or it would become irrelevant. Is he right? Will Christianity become irrelevant? Is the anxious "sky is falling" talk warranted? Should immense anxiety be allowed to consume anyone claiming the name of Jesus? I do not believe so. Quite the opposite, as we will discover from our study of the book of Esther. The story of the book of Esther takes place in a time in the Jewish people's history where it seemed that they were going to face an end to their beliefs and their way of life, and ultimately to their worship of the One True God. However, the pieces of the puzzle scattered on the board of history in Esther 1–2 ultimately brought God much glory as he showed his power over kings, kingdoms, and all people. Esther is a book that has God as the main character, though he is never mentioned. It is the book whose message practically demands us to stop worrying, he reigns.

THE MESS OF PUZZLE PIECES

As a kid, I loved putting puzzles together, and now my oldest daughter has also taken an interest in puzzles. When she first gets the puzzle out and pours the pieces on the floor, it looks like a giant mess. Puzzle pieces are everywhere, and at first glance they have no coherent sense about them. It is amazing to watch my daughter work the puzzle and put the pieces together. She is very methodical and strategic. She will always start with the corner pieces and match up other pieces, using the box as a guide. As I watch her organize the pieces with the picture on the box, it reminds me that this is what God is doing in the world, and it is what he did in the book of Esther. God has decreed what will transpire, and he sovereignly puts the pieces of people's actions, both sinful and not, in their places to accomplish his before-time purpose to present a picture that displays his glory to the world.

Many times, in our own lives, we may have asked the following questions of God: "Why are you doing this? Why has this happened? Why is this going on?" You look at the choices of people in positions of influence and power. You observe the choices of people in various parts of our culture. We look at the scattered puzzle pieces of human actions in our society today and think, what in the world is going on? How can God be in control? Everything is just one big mess of puzzle pieces. Just think about it. Would you say things are in order today in our country? A trillion dollars in debt, morality is increasingly being redefined. Sexual immorality is celebrated. Millions of babies have been murdered in their mother's womb. In the first two chapters of the book of Esther, a mess of puzzle pieces (sinful actions wrought by sinful men and women) are cast out on the table of life with seemingly no coherent reason to it. However, as Esther progresses, the pieces come together to form a beautiful picture of God's glory in his people's redemption. We will see the pieces being put together as we move through this book.

THE BOOK OF ESTHER

The book of Esther helps us to understand God's ways and workings with a fallen world filled with fallen people. Remember, this is a book which does not mention the name of God once. To say that this is strange is an understatement. For any book written in this time period to not mention things such as sacrifices, prayers, rituals, or God's name is just abnormal.[1] By not mentioning God's name, the author is making the point that God is everywhere in the background of this book.[2] The main character of the book of Esther is not Mordecai, Esther, Haman, or Xerxes. Actually, the main character is God, and the book teaches us about God's hidden providence. We learn about God's hidden hand guiding and moving circumstances of life. God works in the choices the people in this book make to accomplish his determined purposes. God sees the end picture, whereas we may be blessed to see some of the pieces put together. God knows how everything is going to turn out and directs the choices of people to his intended end. God is in control of it. He even decrees it. He sees the beautiful picture of history and how it points people to his glory. He alone has that view. He alone is outside of time, and yet dwells in time at the

1. Tomasino, "Esther," 472.
2. Tomasino, "Esther," 472.

same time. We do not have that luxury. Books like Esther help us to understand that God reigns over human affairs for his glory, which should propel us toward faithfulness wherever in history we find ourselves.

It is also striking that, in this book, God uses two not-so-perfect Jews. Have you ever heard that Esther was a heroine? This is not completely true. She has been disobedient to God's commands. She ate food she was not supposed to eat. She did not seem to have any desire to go to the homeland, as per the instructions of God. She is not portrayed like Daniel. Mordecai, her uncle and father figure, is a liar. He hides his identity. They are not picture-perfect examples of what it means to be "godly." They are not the heroes of the story. God is. Ironically enough, you and I are not the heroes of our own story either. Jesus is. In the book of Esther, you have these two imperfect Jews who are not faithfully adhering to God's commands as they live in the Persian kingdom. There is also this man named Haman, who is a leader in the Persian government. Haman rises up against the Jews to eradicate the Jews because he hates them. He is an Amalekite, and the Amalekites were ancient enemies of the Jews (1 Sam 15; Exod 17:14). God uses Esther and Mordecai to save the Jewish people, and even to eradicate the Jews' enemies. It is a beautiful picture of how God works in the everyday circumstances of life to achieve his redemptive purposes.

THE PUZZLE PIECES OF ESTHER 1

The book of Esther begins in verses 1–2: "Now it took place in the days of Ahasuerus, the Ahasuerus who reigned from India to Ethiopia over 127 provinces, in those days as King Ahasuerus sat on his royal throne which was at the citadel in Susa."[3] Most translations of Scripture identify the king of this story as Ahasuerus, which is the Hebrew transliteration of his name.[4] The Greek transliteration of

---

3. Unless otherwise noted, all Scripture references are in the NASB translation.

4. Baldwin, "Esther," 446.

his name is Xerxes.[5] Xerxes ruled from 486–465 BC, and was the son of Darius and grandson of Cyrus the Great.[6] He is famous for his invasion of Greece, as depicted by Herodotus, who wrote the *The Persian Wars* in 445 BC.[7] Perhaps you have heard the story of the three hundred Spartans who fought against the Persians and stood them off?

Xerxes is a prideful, haughty, wicked man. He is irrational, sensual, immoral, and cruel. His rule, as seen in verses 1–2, covers a vast part of the known world. At that time, this would have been the largest empire to date.

In verse 3, during the third year of his reign, Xerxes gave a banquet for all his nobles and officials. He invited all the military officers of Persia and Medea, as well as the princes and nobles of the provinces. Verse 4 tells us this feast lasts for 180 days! Xerxes filled the days by putting on a display of his wealth and splendor. The riches of Persia were legendary. Heredotus reports that Darius received over fourteen thousand talents of gold and silver as annual tribute.[8] It is estimated that Alexander the Great gathered 180,000 talents of gold and silver from his conquest of Persia.[9] A Greek talent is approximately fifty-seven pounds.[10] That is a lot of gold and silver. Xerxes is displaying his wealth and preparing to invade the Greeks. His father, Darius, wanted to destroy Greece and never accomplished this goal before his death, and Xerxes had to wait three years to get this invasion of Greece started because Egypt and Babylon had rebelled against him.[11] He sees that the time has now come, and he calls all his officials to Susa to plan a massive invasion. They strategize how they will take Greece and, at the end of the 180-day summit, they have a seven-day festival which is described in verses 5–8. It was basically a week-long drinking party.

5. Baldwin, "Esther," 446.

6. Tomasino, "Esther," 470.

7. Tomasino, "Esther," 472.

8. Tomasino, "Esther," 474.

9. Tomasino, "Esther," 474.

10. Tomasino, "Esther," 474.

11. Tomasino, "Esther," 470.

Normally, the Persians insisted that their guests drink nonstop, but Xerxes does not require perpetual drinking at this festival.[12] His main wife, Queen Vashti, was at the same time hosting a party for the women in verse 9.[13] The Persians were partiers. They loved their wine. In verse 6, the author gives a picture of the setting where the banquet/party took place. They describe the setting of this party as a courtyard that was beautifully decorated with white cotton curtains and blue hangings, which were fastened with linen chords and purple ribbons to silver rings embedded in marble pillars. Gold and silver couches stood in the mosaic pavement of porphyry, marble, pearl, and other costly stones. Drinks were served in golden goblets of unique designs. There was an abundance of royal wine, reflecting the king's generosity. No limits were placed on the drinking, for the king had instructed all his palace officials to serve each man as much as he wanted.

A QUEEN'S REFUSAL AND A KING'S VENGEANCE

I'm the first Christian in my family, and I was not redeemed by the grace of God through faith in the LORD Jesus until around age twenty-three. Looking back, many of my poor decisions in life (and yes, there are many) can be traced to times when I was under the influence of alcohol. Xerxes, emboldened by the bottle, makes a rash decision in verses 10–11. Here Xerxes orders Queen Vashti to come to his banquet in order to display her beauty for all to marvel at. The Bible says that his heart is merry with wine. He is intoxicated and orders Queen Vashti to come before his throne. Jewish traditions taught that Xerxes commanded Vashti to put her crown on and appear naked before a bunch of drunk men.[14] Whether that is true or not is not the ultimate point. It is evident that Xerxes is arrogantly asking his wife to do something she felt

12. Tomasino, "Esther," 477.
13. Martin, "Esther," 702.
14. Tomasino, "Esther," 478.

was degrading. The queen responds in verse 12 by essentially saying "No!"

The King's Response

Xerxes does not take kindly to Vashti's refusal. He is used to always getting his way, and he is embarrassed from being rejected by his Queen. Xerxes, brimming with fury at this point, brings in his wise men to advise him how to handle Vashti per the law in Esther 1:13–15. He brings his trusted seven princes and asks, "According to law, what is to be done with Queen Vashti, because she did not obey the command of King Ahasuerus delivered by the eunuchs?" One of the king's servants speaks up in verses 16–20:

> For the queen's conduct will become known to all the women causing them to look with contempt on their husbands by saying, "King Ahasuerus commanded Queen Vashti to be brought in to his presence, but she did not come." This day the ladies of Persia and Media who have heard of the queen's conduct will speak in the same way to all the king's princes, and there will be plenty of contempt and anger. If it pleases the king, let a royal edict be issued by him and let it be written in the laws of Persia and Media so that it cannot be repealed, that Vashti may no longer come into the presence of King Ahasuerus, and let the king give her royal position to another who is more worthy than she. When the king's edict which he will make is heard throughout all his kingdom, great as it is, then all women will give honor to their husbands, great and small.

You have to chuckle a little at this. The servants of the king are mainly concerned with how women in the empire will began to defy their husbands because of Vashti's example. If this should go unpunished, they presume that their wives and other husband's wives in the empire will refuse their unreasonable demands. This is a patriarchal society where women were expected to subject themselves unconditionally to their husbands.[15] These men do not want any change in that system of thought. The king responds in verses 21–22 by basically saying, "You are right, Vashti should not enter my presence again. She will lose her position as queen and we are going to send a letter throughout all 127 provinces telling them that the man is the master of his household." The letter is sent throughout all the empire, heralding men as masters. I hope at this point you are rolling your eyes. Anyone who says that mankind is generally good really needs a good whiff of Persian history or even to take a moment to study any era or age in the history of mankind.

Why?

Why is God allowing Xerxes to act like a pagan buffoon? Why allow such cruel silliness in the Persian Empire? Why are all of these things happening? How can a good God allow all these wicked things to happen? We have to put the pieces together to begin seeing what God is doing. Vashti is taken from her position and can no longer see the king again, ever. All the men in Persia are declared to be the masters of their own home and we make our way to chapter 2 of Esther. How can a good God allow these wicked works to win the day? We will come back to this question later in this chapter and throughout the book.

ESTHER 2: MORE PUZZLE PIECES

Between the last verse of Esther 1 and the first verse of Esther 2, approximately four years has passed. Xerxes invaded Greece and failed. He took his army and went into Greece and sacked Athens, but at great cost. Xerxes, with the greatest army in history, invades Greece, and a few Greeks continue to push them back until they annihilate Xerxes's navy, and he has to go back to Persia

15. Tomasino, "Esther," 479.

defeated and humiliated.[16] This is where chapter 2 began. Xerxes is back in Persia and needed a distraction. Therefore, around 478 BC, he began a lengthy search process to replace Vashti.[17] Xerxes's anger had subsided, and he remembered Vashti and her beauty. He remembered the decree and the permanence of it. When the Persians issued a decree, it could not be reversed.[18] This policy, most likely, was meant to force the Persian kings to greatly think through decrees before they were issued as laws. Xerxes misses his former queen and her physical beauty. He cannot get her back. He is distraught because of the massive losses to his army and the failed invasion in Greece. He does not know what to do. However, one of his young advisors has an idea in verses 2–4a. He stated,

> Then the king's attendants, who served him, said, "Let beautiful young virgins be sought for the king. Let the king appoint overseers in all the provinces of his kingdom that they may gather every beautiful young virgin to the citadel of Susa, to the harem, into the custody of Hegai, the king's eunuch, who is in charge of the women; and let their cosmetics be given them. Then let the young lady who pleases the king be queen in place of Vashti."

This young advisor appeals to Xerxes's lust to give him encouragement. He recommends Xerxes gather up all the available virgins throughout the empire and pick the one that pleases him the most. A virgin means a woman of marrying age in this context.[19] Xerxes heartily agrees. This is the distraction he wanted, and Xerxes has all the most beautiful women that Persia has to offer gathered up to bring them all to his harem. A harem in the original language means "a house of women," a special quarters reserved for the king's wives and concubines.[20] All the women Xerxes gathered up instantly became his concubines, yet one of them was to become his queen.

16. Smith, *Minor Prophets*, 476.

17. Smith, *Minor Prophets*, 476.

18. Baldwin, "Esther," 446.

19. Tomasino, "Esther," 480.

20. Tomasino, "Esther," 481.

We Meet Mordecai and Esther

First impressions are important. Whether it is for a job interview or a social outing of sorts, a great first impression goes a long way. In 2:5 and 7, we meet a Jewish man in the fortress of Susa whose name was Mordecai, son of Jair from the tribe of Benjamin, and we meet Hadassah, the daughter of Mordecai's uncle, who is called Esther. In verse 7, our first impression of Esther is painted clearly for our minds to comprehend. The author describes Esther in the following terms: "Now the young lady was beautiful of form and face, and when her father and her mother died, Mordecai took her as his own daughter." Her beauty is such that she catches the eye of the king's officials, and she is invited into the king's harem in verse 8. Esther is pleasing to the king's official, named Hegai, who is entrusted with bringing in the women, and she wins his favor in verse 9. Hegai advances her to the best place in the harem and gives her provisions. Is this a coincidental or providential piece of the puzzle? Our first impression of Esther is that she is beautiful and winsome. Yet we see another side of her in verse 10. She intentionally hides her national identity, which she is told to do by Mordecai in order to have a better shot at being made queen. Mordecai, in verse 11, checked on her each day. She is eating Persian food and enjoying the life of a Persian concubine. Now, that may not sound like a bad thing, but is it really good for one under the Old Testament dietary law to do such a thing?

In chapter 1 of the book of Daniel, he was brought into Babylon and refused to eat the king's food. Why? Daniel did not want to eat unclean food, per the law of Moses (the first five books of Old Testament). He loved God and would not push aside the word of the Lord in any circumstance. This was consistently true of Daniel throughout his life, as recorded in the book known by his name in Scripture. Esther, whether through ignorance or willful disobedience, is living as a Persian rather than a covenant follower of God. She seems to be neglecting God's dietary commands in the law of Moses. Think about it. What does she do throughout the narrative thus far? Did she say, "I'm going to follow God no matter what" or

"I'm going to be faithful to his commands no matter what"? No. She feasts on the food forbidden in Scripture. She willfully goes into the harem. She hides her Jewish identity from the government official over the harem. Does she sound like a faithful follower of God? Did you know that the Jews had been commanded by God, after Cyrus the Great had risen in the power, to go back to Jerusalem? So here are Esther and Mordecai, and they are willfully living in disobedience to God's call to go back to Jerusalem (Jeremiah 29:10, Ezra 1–5). Esther is seeking to be queen instead of seeking God. Yet even in Esther and Mordecai's disobedience, God is faithful.

Now Wait a Moment

Wait a moment! I can see some Sunday School teacher's blood boiling at such an accusation. Esther unfaithful? Was it wrong for her to stay back? Well, even if it was not wrong for her to stay back, there is no doubt that it was against God's word for her to eat unclean food and engage in unlawful activities. Now, we can sympathize with her to some degree. Imagine being a young woman in a pagan empire, scared for your life, and there is a lot of anti-Semitism that seemingly exists in Persia, per the rest of the book of Esther. You have an opportunity to have a wealthy, comfortable life, and you take it. All that is required is to hide your cultural identity and religious beliefs. Daniel refused such a compromise, yet Esther made it. She is not faithful; rather, she is fearful.

Before we stand with a self-righteous eye toward Esther or are unduly critical of her, let us ask ourselves some questions. How many of us have compromised the truth of God for convenience and advancement? How many of us have an imperfect track record, like Esther? How many of us have failed God? How many of us know the commands of God and still struggle to do them? All of us. Every single one of us who claim to follow the LORD Jesus has struggled with obedience. We all struggle with faithfulness. Rather than demean Esther, we should see ourselves in her. The most encouraging part of Esther and this book is that our faithfulness does not determine the success of God's mission to save and deliver his people. God accomplishes his purposes whether we are faithful or not. Does that give us an excuse? No. On the contrary, true success as God's redeemed is faithfulness to him.

FAITHFULNESS IS SUCCESS

Faithfulness is success, but the fame, influence, power, or wealth a person has are not Biblical measures of success. These are worldly measures of success, and ultimately those who are greatest in the kingdom of God are generally not in those categories (1 Cor 1:25–27). They are the redeemed of God, who faithfully are serving the LORD Jesus in all that he has called them to do. In Matthew 25:14–30, Jesus outlines this truth in a parable. In Matthew 25:14–30, Jesus tells a story of a man with three servants. One servant was entrusted with five talents, another with two talents, and the third servant with one talent. The man had entrusted all he had to the servants and left on a journey. The servant with five talents immediately went to work and made five more talents. The servant with two talents also doubled his initial talent entrustment. However, the servant with one talent buried it in the sand. The man comes back, and he says the exact same thing to both the servant with the ten talents and the servant with the four talents. He told them, in verses 21 and 23, the following: "Well done, good and faithful slave. You were faithful with a few things, I will put you in charge of many things; enter into the joy of your master." Notice that their commendation was the same, although their fruitfulness was not equal. Faithfulness to be a good steward of what had been entrusted to them was success before the master. The servant who buried his talent in the sand was cast from the master's presence as he proved his disloyalty toward his master by his actions. The point here is profound. The redeemed of God are called to faithfully serve God with what they have been entrusted. The ends do not justify the means. The means matter. Success as God's people is faithfulness to God and his word.

Back to Esther 2

One of the best movies I saw as a kid growing up was *Back to the Future*. The premise was of the main character, Marty McFly, accidentally going thirty years in the past through the DeLorean time-machine car. While stuck in the past, he comes into contact with his parents before they were married. Throughout the whole movie, Marty is trying to right some wrongs as well as get back to the future. Let us for a moment go back in time to Esther 2:12 to examine the rest of the chapter before we go back to the future to understand the implications of the truths we uncover.

In verse 12, Esther undergoes a year of beatification, and in verse 13 she is given a choice before she goes to the king. This is her one shot to impress Xerxes. The official, whose favor she has, gives her some advice, which she takes. Esther, per verse 9, is taken into the king's harem, which means she is a concubine at this point. In Persia, as elsewhere in the ancient world, concubines usually came into their marriage without ceremony and did not possess the same rights and responsibilities as full-fledged wives.[21] The ancient requirement for becoming a concubine was simply beauty.[22] As the king's concubine, Esther is summoned and only brings what her caretaker, whose favor she has won, told her to bring. Esther, a Jewish woman and now a concubine, is brought before the king to entertain him and give him whatever he may ask for. In Esther 16:2, she is taken to King Xerxes at the royal palace during early winter of the seventh year of his reign, four years after Esther 1. The king loved Esther, per verse 17, more than any of the other women. He delighted in her, overtaken by her natural beauty, and he set the royal crown on her head, declaring her queen instead of Vashti.

Esther had one night with the king to impress him, and the king is enthralled with her. She gives herself to a pagan king, which is not a trait that the Bible is putting forth as admirable. However, in the pages of Scripture we find the real stories of real people

21. Tomasino, "Esther," 484–85.
22. Tomasino, "Esther," 484–85.

and the faithful covenant God, who redeemed them and renewed them. The king is impressed with her humility and her beauty, and he delights in her more than all the four hundred virgins that have come before him. In verse 18, the king proclaimed throughout all the land that there was to be a remission of taxes and the distribution of royal gifts, all in honor of Queen Esther. Notice how earthy the details of this story feel. It seems as if we are reading something out of a history textbook in social studies class. That is the point. Do you think this is happening by accident? Do you think all these events are happening by circumstance? There is a God behind these events, using even the flaws of Esther and Mordecai, to bring about his perfect plan to deliver the Jewish people for his glory and fame. The point the Scriptural author is increasingly going to make for us who read this book is that God rules over the everyday details of this world. We see that point come out further as the story shifts in verse 19 to Mordecai and his report of a plot against the king.

Another Piece of the Puzzle: Mordecai Reports a Plot Against the King

Mordecai, who is an official of Xerxes's kingdom, is at the king's gate, where important kingdom business is discussed, and he hears of a plot in verse 21 and exposes the plot to Esther. Esther responds to the information given to her by Mordecai by telling the king of the plot on behalf of Mordecai. The allegation is investigated, and those who sought to do the king harm were hanged on the gallows. Mordecai's report of the plot is recorded in the chronicles of Persia in the presence of the king. This event may seem unimportant at first glance, but it later fits into the puzzle pieces which profoundly come together with regard to God's deliverance of the Jews.

God is putting together the pieces of the puzzle to deliver the Jews out of the hand of a man named Haman, who is going to come on the scene soon. God is using the mistakes, the circumstances, and the choices of a wicked king like Xerxes. He is using the mistakes of Esther and Mordecai's lying to accomplish his good purposes. God is sovereign over every detail of the actions of people in this world. The acts of rebellion against God are even used (though often unknown to us) for God's good purpose and decrees. Whether we are faithful or unfaithful, God's purposes will be accomplished. God's glory is the point of history, not us. Our call as his people is to be faithful to him, knowing that it is only his Son who can change the world with finality.

HOW DOES A GOOD GOD RULE OVER AN EVIL WORLD?

God is good all the time, and all the time God is good. I have heard that so often in church settings and amongst God's people. Upfront, I believe it to be a 100 percent true that God is good all the time and all the time God is good. However, we live in a dark world filled to the brim with rebellion against its Creator; a world where millions of babies in our country have been aborted. Since 1973, we have killed/aborted approximately more than fifty-nine million babies (which could be much higher depending on which statistic you use). We live in a country where the highest court went against the God-ordained institution of marriage as being defined as a covenant between a man and a woman. We live in a world where little girls are sold into sex slavery and little boys are sold as slave labor to harsh masters. We live in a world of pestilence, war, destruction, rape, murder, etc. The following question must be asked: If God is good and he is in control, then why so much evil? Why so much evil in Esther chapters 1 and 2? In this puzzle, there are four corner puzzle pieces that we must put into place before we are able to see the answer to such a question.

THE FOUR CORNER PIECES OF THE HISTORY PUZZLE

When working on a puzzle, the first step is to find the corner pieces and put them in place. The four corner pieces form the outline with which to put the puzzle together to ultimately see a picture come forth. There are four important corner pieces to put in their place so we can begin to make sense of God's goodness and sovereign rule in a fallen world. They are: 1) God is holy; 2) evil exists because humankind exists; 3) the solution to the problem of evil is Jesus; and 4) God is working in all things for our good and his glory.

First Corner Piece: God is Holy.

In Isaiah 6, the prophet Isaiah is taken up to the throne room of God, where his manifest presence is. God's glory is brightly on display as Isaiah sees God lifted high and exalted. The angels are praising God, saying in Isaiah 6:3, "And one called out to another and said, "Holy, Holy, Holy, is the LORD of hosts, The whole earth is full of His glory." Notice that the angels are saying, "Holy, Holy, Holy." The word "holy" means "separate" or "other." God is in a category separate and other than all the cosmos. The angels are singing the truth and reality of God, that he is altogether in a different category than all beings in the Cosmos. God is the only being who is all-powerful, eternal, all-knowing, omnipresent, and perfect in all his attributes. He transcends time and space. He is majestic and perfectly pure. He is perfectly righteous and flawless in executing his justice. It is God's otherness that brings Isaiah to the point of being totally undone. Isaiah falls on his face and says, "woe to me, I'm a man with unclean lips and I live amongst a people who are unclean." God responds by atoning for the source of Isaiah's sin, which Isaiah named, through the altar of sacrifice. The first and foremost thing we must understand about how a good God interacts in a fallen world is to see that God's goodness and otherness is simply awesome. God is truly wondrous to behold.

Second Corner Piece: Evil Exists because Humankind Exists.

The second corner piece is that the reason evil exists is because we as humankind exist. The reason there are abortions, sexual immorality, war, human trafficking, pestilence, famine, disease, heartache, hurt, and all other sin is the result of our existence in this world. Romans 5:12 states, "Through one man sin entered into the world, and death through sin, and so death spread to all men, because all sinned." Adam, the first man, sinned, and we inherited his sinful nature as well as his guilt. Therefore, it is natural for us to do things that are contrary to our good and to the glory of God. It comes naturally to us. Our desires are in rebellion against God and our will freely follows our desires. It is easy for us. Per the Scripture we sin because we are sinners. We are not sinners because we sin. We do what is naturally in our heart. Romans 3:23 makes it clear that this is the condition of all humankind. The passage states, "for all have sinned and fall short of the glory of God." Your sin may manifest itself differently than others. However, make no mistake—you and I are natural rebels against our Creator. Though some of our sins may be private and hidden, before God they are ever-present. God is holy and we are wicked. We all covet, lust, hate, have jealousy, are envious and manipulative, and lie, just to name a few sins. If you want to know what God thinks about mankind apart from his Holy Spirit and grace, then Genesis 6:5 is the place to go. This passage states, "Then the LORD saw that the wickedness of man was great on the earth, and that every intent of the thoughts of his heart was only evil continually." This is a diagnosis of mankind. Is it a good one? No, but it is accurate. God looks on mankind and says, "They are a mess." The reason death, disease, human trafficking, abortion, famine, and sexual immorality exist is because we exist and are in a state of rebellion against our Creator. We are wicked.

Today, it is popular to make the statement "they are a good person" or "I'm a good person." Have you ever noticed people who say "I'm a good person" can only make that claim in comparison to others around them or in the society to which they belong? God's word calls us to not compare ourselves amongst each other to determine our goodness, but to compare ourselves to God's standard of righteousness. When we do that, the word "good" is the last description we can attach to ourselves if we are being honest examiners. You and I are wicked. Esther was wicked. Mordecai was wicked. Xerxes was wicked. Xerxes's wickedness manifested itself in different sins. He was a drunkard and a sexually immoral person. Mordecai and Esther's sin nature manifests itself in lying and compromise. This puzzle piece is key to understanding history. A lot of people will brashly respond to all this and say, "Well, why doesn't God do something about evil?" That is a dangerous proposition. Think about the flood in Genesis 6–7. If God did away with evil, not one person would be breathing today. God's common grace is why life has persisted on. Remember, the problem with our world is not the God who created it good, but the creatures who made it bad.

Third Corner Piece: The Solution to Evil is Jesus

God is both perfectly just and perfectly merciful. How can a just God completely dispense flawless justice and mercy at the same time? How can a perfectly merciful God not work at the expense of justice? This was the tension when God spoke to Moses in Exodus 34:6–7:

> Then the LORD passed by in front of him and proclaimed,
> "The LORD, the LORD God, compassionate and gracious,
> slow to anger, and abounding in lovingkindness and
> truth; who keeps lovingkindness for thousands, who
> forgives iniquity, transgression and sin; yet He will by no
> means leave the guilty unpunished, visiting the iniquity
> of fathers on the children and on the grandchildren to
> the third and fourth generations.

The third corner piece of the puzzle that is crucial to grasp as the everlasting solution to the problem of evil is the person and work of the LORD Jesus. He is the resolution of the perceived tension between God's mercy toward his people and his just punishment of sin. It is the mystery hidden in past ages and generations, but now revealed to God's people (Col 1:26). The gospel of the LORD Jesus is God's solution to evil.

Galatians 4:4-5 states, "But when the fullness of the time came, God sent forth his Son, born of a woman, born under the Law, so that He might redeem those who were under the Law, that we might receive the adoption as sons." When the fullness of time came, God sent forth his Son, born under the law, so that he might redeem those who are under the law. The law highlights our imperfection before God, exposing our dark deeds and deceitful hearts. Jesus came into this world so that we would be forgiven, reconciled to God the Father, and adopted into his family. History and its pinnacle climax centers on Jesus and his cross in the little region of the world known as Palestine. At the perfect time in history, Jesus came as God's everlasting solution to the problem of evil.

God, through the LORD Jesus, deals with the problem of evil because he upholds his justice and gives his love. Jesus, living the sinless life we could never dream of pursuing or living out, earned for us righteousness. Jesus lived under the law in his humanity and is the only person who obeyed the law completely. Jesus obeyed every ordinance and every law perfectly before God in every moment with every attitude. Every word uttered and every intent was flawless before God the Father. The life of Jesus was perfect, sinless, and holy in all his thirty-three years on earth. His obedience to God in all its perfections culminated with his voluntary death on a cross, whereby he endured the judgment of God for the sins of God's people. His resurrection on the third day was validation of his identity as God incarnate and the sinless Savior, who alone brings the forgiveness of sin through his death on the cross. The LORD Jesus' perfect work on the cross was the climax of history. Everything in history points to it or points back to it. Jesus is the solution for evil. You see, in Christ, God reconciles all those who will repent and believe; all the while, God upholds his perfect justice (Rom 1:16-17). Jesus was punished by God for our sin. God will also punish those who reject Jesus with everlasting wrath in a terrifying place called hell (2 Thess 1:8–9). History points toward Jesus. Esther points toward Jesus. God is saving the Jewish people to ultimately bring forth his Son and redeem those from every people group in the world. Jesus is the climax and center of history. He is the solution. It is to him that the story in Esther ultimately points. Paul describes the work of Jesus in powerful terms in 2 Corinthians 5:21: "He made Him who knew no sin to be sin on our behalf, so that we might become the righteousness of God in Him." God imputed the sin of his people to Jesus upon the cross, and God ascribes the LORD Jesus' perfect life, his righteousness, to our account before God.

I heard a great illustration of the truth of 2 Corinthians 5:21, though I do not remember its exact source. The illustration goes something like this: there was a school teacher who taught a very difficult math course. He had twenty students, nineteen of which never got a passing score on any of the homework, quizzes, or tests. All the students had gradebooks filled with F's except one student, who was the ultimate curve killer. He got straight A's. This student never missed a question in all the homework, quizzes, and tests. Now, the teacher desired for the students to pass the course, and so he forgave all their F's. He removed all the F's from each of the nineteen student's names in the gradebook, yet the students still could not pass the course. If there were no grades next to their names, then there was no merit by which they could pass the math course. So the professor took the grades of the student who had straight A's and gave them to all the other nineteen students. That is a picture of what God does for his people in the Jesus Christ. In the LORD Jesus, God the Father took away all our F's before him, and God the Father gave his people all the LORD Jesus' A's. When God looks upon you, if you have trusted in Jesus, your sins are forgiven, and judicially you are clothed with his perfect record before God, his righteousness. We are purified with his righteousness. That is the gospel. By grace you are saved through faith, and that faith lays ahold of the work of the LORD Jesus Christ. His shed blood covers our sins and his life is imputed to our account. Amazing grace!

Where do you stand with God's solution to evil? Have you owned your true state before God, as a rebel who deserves eternal death and trusted in the LORD Jesus' merit alone to save you from the punishment that is rightly yours? Is Jesus the center of your life? The glory of Jesus is the climax of history, but is it the climax of your personal history? He is the only solution to the evil of the world and the evil of every human soul. Jesus saves his people and, by his Spirit, changes us from the inside out as we await the day of our perfection in his presence forever procured by his cross.

Fourth Corner Piece: God is at Work in All the Details for His Glory

The fourth and final corner piece of the puzzle to understanding God's goodness in light of an evil world is to grasp the reality that the actions of others may have been intended for evil, but God ultimately works in it for good, particularly the good of his people to the praise of his Name. This glorious truth is seen in the life of Joseph the son of Jacob in Genesis 37–50. Joseph the favorite son of Jacob is betrayed by his brothers and sold into slavery. He succeeds for a season in the house of his master in Egypt, but then is falsely accused of a crime which lands him in an Egyptian prison. Hope seems to have passed, and his life looks bleak. However, God— through Joseph's interpretation of the dream of two servants of the pharaoh and ultimately the pharaoh himself—is moved to the position of second in command of all of Egypt. God uses Joseph to preserve the life of his family and the lives of families in Egypt during a terrible seven-year famine that was preceded by seven years of plenty. Joseph is reconciled to his brothers and forgives them freely. Joseph's brothers, after their father's death, struggle with fear about Joseph taking revenge, and they seek his forgiveness once more. Joseph's response in Genesis 50:20 is this: "As for you, you meant evil against me, but God meant it for good in order to bring about this present result, to preserve many people alive." The actions of Joseph's brother were evil, but God was sovereignly

21

working through the evil acts of Joseph's brothers for a greater good, the deliverance of many people from death and destruction.

Another example of this is in the book of Acts. In Acts 4, Peter and John are arrested and put before the very counsel that killed the LORD Jesus. They refuse to stop speaking of Jesus and are eventually set free. They go to the church and the church goes to God in prayer. The church's prayer contains some powerful truth. The church states in Acts 4:27–28, "For truly in this city there were gathered together against Your holy servant Jesus, whom You anointed, both Herod and Pontius Pilate, along with the Gentiles and the peoples of Israel, to do whatever Your hand and Your purpose predestined to occur." The church conveyed that Pontius Pilate, Herod, and the Jews all made freely evil choices to kill Jesus, but God determined from eternity past to use their freely evil choices for the most glorious good ever conceived, the salvation of sinners by the sacrifice of the LORD Jesus. God uses the actions of men and women in his allowing will to achieve his purposes in his decreed will, which is God's providence. God's providence is his reign over all things, guiding all things through to God's determined end all for his everlasting praise (Ps 103:19). The truth that God is all-knowing, all-powerful, fully everywhere at all times demands that God providentially rule the world (1 John 3:20; Job 42:2; Acts 17:28). God's very nature upholds the doctrine that God reigns over all the details of his creation and uses the fallen state of man to achieve his decrees in history for his name sake. We will examine this concept further in this book with this definition of providence here in mind (chapter 3–4).

Take a moment and really ponder how God was working in Esther 1–2. Xerxes chose to get rid of Vashti. He made that choice, and he is accountable for it. Mordecai and Esther also chose to hide Esther's Jewish identity. But God was working in those things to accomplish his purposes, which he decreed from eternity past. He was working in the choices of both Esther and Xerxes to bring about the deliverance of the Jews from annihilation. God uses the choices of men and women to accomplish his good purposes. He is sovereign over all. He is outside of time. God's plans cannot be stopped or thwarted. When we see evil, when we see heartache and hurt, we may not be able to see past chapters 1 and 2 in our lives, but remember that there are chapters 3–10 coming that explains it all. We are called to entrust ourselves to the Triune God who reigns. That is the message of the book of Esther. Many of us in pridefully want all the answers now. We live in the Google age where all the information we could ever want is at our fingertips. However, God is not Google. His decreed purposes unfold per his time for his fame.

Therefore, we as followers of the LORD Jesus are called to rest in God and live out the call to stop worrying, for he reigns. To do that, we must see clearly the four corner pieces of the history puzzle, which are: 1) God is holy; 2) evil exists because humankind exists; 3) the solution to the problem of evil is Jesus; and 4) God is working in all things for the church's good and his glory. Those four corner pieces are foundational to putting together the puzzle of God's redemptive masterpiece, displaying his glory in all of human history.

DISCUSSION QUESTIONS:

1. Who is Xerxes? Who are Esther and Mordecai, and how does the author describe them?

2. How did Esther rise to become the queen, and how was her ascension unique?

3. What is divine providence?

4. What are the four corner puzzle pieces we must grasp in order to understand God's work in the world?

5. What does the phrase "God is holy" mean? How does a holy God rule a fallen world?

6. Where do you stand with God's solution to the problem of evil?

2

How Does This Make Sense?
(Esther 3–4)

IT IS SO BAD today! The world is just going down the drain! I have heard so many people in Christian circles assert those type of ideas by making comments like "Jesus must be coming back very soon, look at how dark our country has become morally" or "If we don't wake up, we are in trouble." When I hear these types of comments, I realize that those who make them are genuinely grieved by the apparent injustice and immorality that looms over our lands. What is happening in our world just does not seem to make any sense. However, in light of history, there were darker ages and days than this. Jesus told us that the church age would be marked by tribulation, wars, immorality, false teaching, etc. (Matt 24:4–13). Immorality and an increasing hostility in some places to Christian truth is not something that should make us shout "the sky is falling"; rather, it is something that Jesus told us we will face (John 15:18–19). Christians across this world face it on a daily basis. There is a woman I know from Africa who believed in the LORD Jesus upon hearing the gospel. Her husband responded by throwing her, as well as her daughter, out to fend for themselves with nothing to their name. God provided in the midst of the messiness of the puzzle pieces of her life. She was able to find work and take care of her daughter. Ultimately, she would later translate the Bible into her native tongue, and now frequently proclaims the gospel in the marketplaces. One day, as she proclaimed the gospel in the marketplace, Boko Haram (an Islamic terrorist group) responded by beating her almost to death. This dear sister in Christ well understands opposition to God's people that has been the norm in history, not something new. It is just a puzzle piece in the historical portrait of God's redemptive work and glory. As we pick back up in Esther 3-4, we will see opposition arise against God's people in the day of Queen Esther.

ESTHER 3: THE PUZZLE PIECE OF OPPOSITION IS PLACED ON THE BOARD.

Let us take a moment to review the important pieces from Esther 1-2 on the puzzle board. God has raised up a young Jewish woman named Esther to become the queen of the Persian empire alongside Xerxes. Her uncle and guardian, Mordecai, has exposed a plot against the king, yet is without reward. Now, in Esther 3-4, the villain of the story is going to be brought forth. The puzzle piece of Haman the Agagite is thrown onto the board, and at first glance does not seem to fit well with any of the existing puzzle pieces. In Esther 3:1, we are told that Xerxes has promoted Haman the Agagite and given him authority over all the princes and officials of his kingdom. Haman is second to Xerxes alone in the kingdom. In Esther 3:2-3, all the officials acknowledge Haman's authority by bowing before him, except one: Mordecai. Haman is made aware of Mordecai's refusal and is filled with rage at Mordecai's refusal to bow in verses 4-5. However, he is not just going to take his vengeance out on Mordecai. Rather, Haman determines to destroy Mordecai and all the Jews in the Persian Empire in verse 6. Haman seeks to annihilate the Jewish people so that all Jewish men, women, and children who breathe are destroyed. Then, in verse 7, Haman superstitiously seeks the timing of the "gods" to seek the Jews' destruction. The word "pur" in this verse is the Babylonian word for "lot," as casting lots was a common method for determining the will of the gods or deciding a matter of great importance in that period of time.[1] Haman is a very superstitious guy. He worships the pagan Babylonian gods and casts lots to determine the most beneficial time for him to approach Xerxes to propose his plan to wipe out the Jews. From his vantage point he wants the pagan gods favor. However, the providence of the One True God is clearly seen in how the lot "pur" falls. For it falls to the last month of the Persian year. As one commentator puts it, "The original readers of this book would have understood that God was working to protect his people even in the timing of events. As things worked out, the Jews had almost a year in which to prepare themselves for the conflict with their enemies."[2] At the end of verse 7, Haman has determined when to approach the king, and next we read his proposal to the king:

> Then Haman said to King Ahasuerus, "There is a certain people scattered and dispersed among the peoples in all the provinces of your kingdom; their laws are different from those of all other people and they do not observe the king's laws, so it is not in the king's interest to let them remain. If it is pleasing to the king, let it be decreed that they be destroyed, and I will pay ten thousand talents of silver into the hands of those who carry on the king's business, to put into the king's treasuries." (Esth 3:8–9)

Haman presents a problem to the king. He portrays the Jews as rebellious and unruly. Being a trusted advisor of the king, Haman uses his position to lie about the Jews and then present in verse 9 a solution for the king: the Jews' destruction and the enhancement of the king's wealth. The ten thousand talents of silver appear to be a bribe. During that time, silver was the monetary standard in Persia.[3] According to the standard for silver established by King Darius, this equals approximately 333 tons of silver, which today

1. Tomasino, "Esther," 488.
2. Martin, "Esther," 705.
3. Martin, "Esther," 706.

would make it a bribe worth about $64 million.[4] However, an even better way to consider the enormity of this bribe is to realize that Haman's bribe, per modern scholarship, is estimated to be approximately two thirds of Persia's annual revenue.[5] Haman is willing to extract all the resources he can from the Jews and perhaps even use silver from his own estate to see to the Jewish people's elimination.

How Does the King Respond to this Blatant Bribe and Perversion of Justice?

The king's response and corresponding decree is the last part of this troubling chapter:

> Then the king took his signet ring from his hand and gave it to Haman, the son of Hammedatha the Agagite, the enemy of the Jews. The king said to Haman, "The silver is yours, and the people also, to do with them as you please." Then the king's scribes were summoned on the thirteenth day of the first month, and it was written just as Haman commanded to the king's satraps, to the governors who were over each province and to the princes of each people, each province according to its script, each people according to its language, being written in the name of King Ahasuerus and sealed with the king's signet ring. Letters were sent by couriers to all the king's provinces to destroy, to kill and to annihilate all the Jews, both young and old, women and children, in one day, the thirteenth day of the twelfth month, which is the month Adar, and to seize their possessions as plunder. A copy of the edict to be issued as law in every province was published to all the peoples so that they should be ready for this day. The couriers went out impelled by the king's command while the decree was issued at the citadel in Susa; and while the king and Haman sat down to drink, the city of Susa was in confusion. (Esth 3:10–15)

4. Tomasino, "Esther," 489.
5. Tomasino, "Esther," 489.

Money talks! The king enthusiastically takes the bribe, recognizing that Haman has the funds to deliver the silver he promised, and allows Haman to decree the destruction of the Jews. Without hestiation, the king takes his signet ring from his hand and gives it to Haman in verse 10. The ring was symbolic of the king's authority. One commentator highlights the importance of the signet ring: "[It] was a symbol of royal authority and in ancient times was used instead of a written signature to seal official documents."[6] This means that the king is giving Haman the authority to execute the solution he proposed concerning the Jews. The king then basically told Haman that he would take the money, and that the people were Haman's to do with as he pleased. Xerxes has just given Haman the authority to do what he wished, confident that every promised piece of silver will be delivered from Haman's own fortune or plundered from the Jews.

In verse 12, the decree is written per Haman's instruction, and in verses 13–14 it is copied and sent out to all of Persia. All the while, in verse 15, Haman and Xerxes sit to drink in luxury with the capital city of Persia in an uproar. Think with me for a moment. Why is this such a grave threat to God's redemptive work? If you recall, Persia covers most of the known world, and Palestine is a conquered territory in the Persian Empire. Remember the Jews who faithfully went back to worship God and rebuild the temple? The Jews in Jerusalem who had returned under previous rulers are included in this. Therefore, on the thirteenth day of the twelfth month, those Jews in Jerusalem are going to be wiped out and destroyed, along with the Jews in all of Persia, which was most of the known world in this period.

This is an all-out assault on God's convenant people. Per Isaiah 53, the Messiah is to come through the Jewish people. He will come out of the line of Judah and David. This is an attack against God's redemptive masterpiece, but as we will see, all of this is actually part of God's redemptive puzzle coming together for his glory.

---

6. Barker and Kohlenberger, *Expositors Bible Commentary*, 733.

WHAT IS TRULY BEHIND THIS ATTACK?
SPIRITUAL WARFARE

In Esther 3, a great threat has arisen to wipe out God's people from dwelling in the earth, who are the recipients of the law, the writings, and the prophets; who were entrusted with the promises of God, which are to find their fulfillment in the LORD Jesus and the new covenant he would bring. A total assault against those who bear God's name has been decreed. Is this just a human coincidence, or is there something more?

In Ephesians 6:10–12, Paul says this:

> Finally, be strong in the LORD and in the strength of His might. Put on the full armor of God, so that you will be able to stand firm against the schemes of the devil. For our struggle is not against flesh and blood, but against the rulers, against the powers, against the world forces of this darkness, against the spiritual forces of wickedness in the heavenly places.

Paul called the church in Ephesus, which found itself in the midst of ancient Asia Minor (modern-day Turkey), to peer behind what was taking place in the opposition and persecution they were facing. He told the church to be strong in the LORD and put on the armor of God because they did not truly struggle with flesh and blood (people), but against the dominion of darkness, namely demonic activity that God allowed to oppose him temporarily. One commentator makes the following observation: "Until the end of this age these demonic forces, already defeated by Christ on the cross, exercise a certain limited authority in temporarily opposing the purposes of God."[7] The irony is that the opposition of these forces is used by God to ultimately fulfill his good purposes. God rules over even those in rebellion against him! This is a topic we will further dive into at the end of chapter 3.

---

7. Barker and Kohlenberger, *Expositors Bible Commentary*, 783.

WHY DOES HAMAN HATE THE JEWS SO MUCH?

Now before we move on, we need to ask why Haman hates the Jewish people so much. We know there is spiritual warfare behind what is transpiring in Haman's actions. However, what is the root motive of Haman to destroy not just Mordecai, but all the Jews? Is it simply petty revenge against Mordecai, or is there something more?

The key to unlocking Haman's hatred is how the Scripture introduces Haman. In Esther 3:1, Haman is called "the Agagite," the son of Hammedatha. Now, what is an Agagite? It is an Amalekite. Jewish tradition considers Haman to have been a descendant of the Amalekite king Agag, an enemy of Israel during Saul's reign (1 Sam 15:7–33).[8] The Amalekites were enemies of the Jews very early on (Exod 17:8–14; Deut 25:17–19). In Israel's early monarch period, Saul failed to destroy the Amalekites completely as God had ordered him to do (1 Sam 15:23).[9] In Deuteronomy 25:17–19, Moses stated,

> Remember what Amalek did to you along the way when you came out from Egypt, how he met you along the way and attacked among you all the stragglers at your rear when you were faint and weary; and he did not fear God. Therefore it shall come about when the LORD your God has given you rest from all your surrounding enemies, in the land which the LORD your God gives you as an inheritance to possess, you shall blot out the memory of Amalek from under heaven; you must not forget.

He tells Israel that, after they conquer the promised land, they are to eventually wipe out the Amalekites. This was God's response to the Amalekite attack against the people of Israel as they were coming out of Egypt. Hundreds of years have passed after the exodus when the first king of Israel, Saul, is given a commission by God in 1 Samuel 15:2–3. Saul is commanded to take Israel's armies and wipe out the Amalekites. Saul partially carries this out

8. Barker and Kohlenberger, *Expositors Bible Commentary*, 732.

9. Barker and Kohlenberger, *Expositors Bible Commentary*, 732.

and leaves King Agag of the Amalekites, and apparently others, alive. Samuel, who was the prophet who anointed Saul, beholds Saul's disobedience and slices up King Agag. Several hundreds of years later, we see a rematch being brought forth between Haman of the Amalekites and Mordecai of the tribe of Benjamin (the same tribe as Saul). These men, as most who lived in ancient antiquity, were very aware of their heritage, and the very fact that Haman is called an Agagite shows that he descends from King Agag himself. Imagine having that type of heritage. Mordecai's refusal to bow just brings to the forefront Haman's hatred toward the Jews. Therefore, his response is basically " I will do what the Amalekites failed to do when Israel was going toward the promise land. I will destroy the Jews through the power of the king of Persia."

The situation is intense. Haman, the second-in-command in the Persian kingdom, plotting the destruction of the Jews because of his intense hatred. Mordecai, in his pride, refused to bow before an ancient enemy of his people. Historically, the Jewish people had no problem with bowing before officials in respect that God had ordained over them, even if they were enemies or other people groups. We see this in Abraham, the father of the Hebrews, in Genesis 23:7 as he bowed before the Hittites. David, in 1 Samuel 24:8, bows before Saul. As a matter of fact, for Mordecai to be an official in the king's government, he had to bow down before Xerxes. Mordecai's refusal to bow is most likely born from pride built off of hundreds of years of animosity. Some Jewish rabbis, in order to cover this up, later stated that Haman actually carried around an idol, and whenever anyone saw Haman they were to bow down to Haman and his idol.[10] However, there is no mention of or evidence for this. The simple fact is that Mordecai refused to bow down before Haman in in Esther 3:2 because he was proud of his heritage. He was proud of being a Jew. He was proud to be of the tribe of Benjamin. As a son of a tribe of Benjamin, he would not bow down to some despicable Amalekite. He just would not do it.

10. Tomasino, "Esther," 488.

A PRINCIPLE IS SEEN HERE

We have come to a stop sign. I remember when my oldest son took one of his driving tests. We arrived at the DMV for him to take his test. He had gotten in the car with the instructor, and I had just sat down in the waiting area. Literally less than a minute later, he and the instructor come back in. I looked at my son and asked, "What happened?" He looked at me, disappointed, and said, "I ran a stop sign." Unfortunately, that was an automatic fail. We do not want to run past this text without stopping to see the principle here. Saul's disobedience in regard to not wiping out the Amalekites had the aftereffect of a very dreadful threat rising against the Jewish people scattered through the Persian Empire. Our present sins have future consequences that affect more people than just us. This is the stop sign we must see and observe: current sin has future consequences.

Have you heard the saying "like father like son, like mother like daughter?" It is amazing how often our children act just like us. This became real to me one day when I was mowing, and my son, three years old at the time, got his little play mower and followed me around the yard, pretending he was mowing just like dad. Our children often take on our characteristics and even take on our patterns of sinful choices. Take, for example, the life of Abraham (the same Abraham who is called the father of all who have faith in verses such as Galatians 3:7), who left his homeland out of faith in God and his promises. Abraham went to a land that he did not know, because God simply called him (Gen 12). However, if you look at Abraham's life carefully, you will see that he was a liar. He was constantly lying. He lied about his wife in Genesis 12:12–13. He does it again in Genesis 20:2. Abraham was quite adept at telling half-truths. Isaac, Abraham's son, is put in a situation in his own life where he has to either protect his wife or protect himself, and guess what he does? He lies about his wife in Genesis 26:6–7 by saying that she is his sister. Isaac later has two sons, Esau and Jacob. Jacob is the younger of the twins, and on the day Esau is supposed to be given the blessing of the family by Isaac, Jacob deceives Isaac to receive the blessing (Genesis 27). As you continue to go forward in time, Genesis tells of Jacob's sons lying to Jacob about Joseph. They sell Joseph, their younger brother, into slavery, but tell Jacob that Joseph was killed by a wild beast and thereby deceived Jacob (Gen 37:18-36). This family lies, deceives, and cheats from generation to generation. The consequences are not only felt in the present, but in the future, as the next generation repeats the patterns set by the previous generation. Our sins affect our current situations in life and future generations.

Now, before despair starts setting in, we are to remind ourselves of the truth Paul forcefully communicates in Romans 7:21—8:1:

> So I find it to be a law that when I want to do right, evil lies close at hand. For I delight in the law of God, in my inner being, but I see in my members another law waging war against the law of my mind and making me captive to the law of sin that dwells in my members. Wretched man that I am! Who will deliver me from this body of death? Thanks be to God through Jesus Christ our LORD! So then, I myself serve the law of God with my mind, but with my flesh I serve the law of sin. There is therefore now no condemnation for those who are in Christ Jesus. For the law of the Spirit of life has set you free in Christ Jesus from the law of sin and death. (ESV)

For those whose faith is in the LORD Jesus alone, the domination of the cycle of sin is broken in Jesus. He delivers us from this body of death, and per Romans 8:1 there is no condemnation in Christ Jesus. In Christ (as noted in Romans 8:2) we are now set free from the law of sin and death. We who God has saved by grace through faith in the finished work of Jesus alone are a forgiven people who are forging forward. The pattern of the domination of sin is broken for all who follow Jesus. Now we, the redeemed, have the privilege of resembling the character of our Father in heaven more each day by God's sanctifying grace alone through the indwelling Holy Spirit (2 Cor 5:7; 1 John 3:1). Ultimately, this is the result of God's amazing love through Jesus, for the testimony of the Christian's new life in Christ is "like Father, like son."

King Saul's disobedience to God in not wiping out the Amalekites resulted in the book of Esther's predicament of possible annihilation for the Jewish people. Mordecai and all God's people are
facing the threat of annihilation. However, opposition is nothing
new for the follower of God, no matter its source.

OPPOSITION WILL COME AS WE SOJOURN IN
THIS FALLEN WORLD

Jesus said, "You will be hated by all because of My name, but it
is the one who has endured to the end who will be saved." Following God, trusting in his promises will lead us into opposition
with the fallen world we all are a part of and live in. Mordecai
responds profoundly in Esther 4:1–2: "When Mordecai learned
all that had been done, he tore his clothes, put on sackcloth and
ashes, and went out into the midst of the city and wailed loudly
and bitterly. He went as far as the king's gate, for no one was to
enter the king's gate clothed in sackcloth." When Mordecai learned
all that had been done concerning the decree to destroy all the
Jews that went out in Susa and throughout the world, he tore his
clothes, put on sackcloth and ashes, and went into the midst of
the city, where he wailed loudly and bitterly. He went as far as the
King's Gate, for no one was to enter the King's Gate clothed in
sackcloth and mourning.[11] Sackcloth was made from goat's hair,
and it was a very coarse material, quite painful to wear.[12] It was a
continual reminder to the one wearing it of their deep distress and
pain. Mordecai was mourning and weeping with great anguish. He
was in pain over the pronouncement of the coming execution of
him and his people. Perhaps his anguish was greater knowing that
it was the result of the past disobedience of his people.

The Jews in the rest of the province react in verse 3 of chapter
4: "In each and every province where the command and decree of
the king came, there was great mourning among the Jews, with

11. Tomasino, "Esther," 490.
12. Tomasino, "Esther," 490.

fasting, weeping and wailing; and many lay on sackcloth and ashes." The tears are flowing and the hearts of the Jews are filled with great shock, anxiety, mourning, and grief at the coming calamity. In verse 4, Esther's maidens and her eunuchs came and told her all that had transpired with Mordecai's behavior, and the queen was in great anguish. Why? Because Mordecai, her adopted father and cousin, is writhing in pain, covered with sackcloth and ashes, and she has no idea what is wrong. She sends clothes to cover Mordecai in verse 4 that he might remove his sackcloth, but he did not accept them. Esther summons the eunuchs and sends them to Mordecai to learn what was going on. He tells the eunuch in verses 5-9, and even gives the eunuch a copy of the edict. Why did Esther not know this was going on? She is the queen. Should not she know these things? Most scholars agree that only 5 percent of Jews could read or write, and that percentage was probably much lower for women.[13] It is possible that Esther could not read and she, being in the king's harem, was isolated from the world. In verse 8, the eunuch explains to her all that has taken place, and tells her of Mordecai's request for her to talk to the king on the Jews' behalf. Esther responds in fear and self-preservation, rather than with courage. Verse 11 conveys Esther's response to Mordecai:

> All the king's servants and the people of the king's provinces know that for any man or woman who comes to the king to the inner court who is not summoned, he has but one law, that he be put to death, unless the king holds out to him the golden scepter so that he may live. And I have not been summoned to come to the king for these thirty days.

Esther's response is one filled with a sense of self-preservation. She basically conveys this message back to Mordecai: "You want me to do what? You want me to go before the king and most likely be killed because he has not summoned me? You want me to go and risk my neck to the king when no servant, no person who goes to the king without an invite, will live? Oh, and Mordecai, the king

13. Tomasino, "Esther," 490.

has not called for me in thirty-one days." Perhaps the king was too busy with his concubines to pay notice to his queen, or maybe she had fallen out of favor with him. Regardless, Esther is not in a good place to go to the king and ask him to spare her people. Notice that she is worried about herself. She is not thinking about God's glory, God's sovereignty, God's truth, God's commands, or God's people. She is thinking that she could die. Anxiety and fear for her own life is what litters her answer back to Mordecai. The encouraging thing is that all of us should be able to relate to Esther here. Whatever trials you may have faced in life or are facing now, we know what it is like to respond in fear and anxiety concerning the outcome of the trials we face.

A Contrast

Daniel is an important figure in the Old Testament Scriptures, living approximately one hundred years before Esther. He is attributed the book of Daniel, whereby we see parts of his life as a faithful follower of the covenant of God, living in pagan Babylon and Persia. In chapter 6 of this book, Daniel is in a situation much like Esther. His life is in danger. A decree from the Persian king went out that no one shall pray to any god but him. Daniel responds by doing what he did every day. He goes to his room and prays to the Holy and Sovereign God of Abraham, Isaac, and Jacob. Unconcerned about the consequences to his life, he cares more about the God his life revolves around. He later gets thrown into a lion's den for his obedience to God and experiences God's deliverance. Daniel is the contrast to Esther. He did not respond with compromise or a desire for self-preservation, but with bold resolve he worshiped the LORD God Almighty resting in God's sovereign care.

Esther does not initially have the same heart as Daniel. She is concerned about her own life. However, let's not be too hard on Esther here. How many of us have compromised when faced with an ethical dilemma? How many of us have chosen self-preservation over doing the right thing per God's word? Sadly, in many ways I identify more with Esther than I do with Daniel. I'm a fallen sinful creature needing the grace of God to not just justify me, but also to sanctify me in the image of Christ. How about you? One of the most beautiful truths about the book of Esther is that God uses fallen people to achieve his great purposes. Have you ever failed God? Have you ever messed up? God uses even our puzzle piece messes to bring about his masterpiece of redemptive glory.

Mordecai's Bold Exhortation

Mordecai's response to Esther is to exhort her to be faithful. Verses 13–14 depict her response: "Do not imagine that you in the king's palace can escape any more than all the Jews. For if you remain silent at this time, relief and deliverance will arise for the Jews from another place and you and your father's house will perish. And who knows whether you have not attained royalty for such a time as this?"

Mordecai proclaims the truth: deliverance will come from somewhere! He knows God will not break his promise to Abraham, Isaac, and Jacob. He is conveying, in faith, that God is sovereignly faithful, and he will deliver. However, Esther will not escape God's judgment if she should walk away from his word. Mordecai encourages her with the reality that perhaps God, in his power and providence, has placed her in the king's harem as queen for this time and this situation, to deliver God's people for God's glory by his providential leading. Mordecai's faith comes out in adversity. He is clinging to the promises of God seen in Holy Scripture. Like Abraham before him, he knows God is trustworthy, and what he has said will not be broken. God has promised that, through Abraham, all the nations will be blessed (Gen 12:3). The Jews will survive, and God's providence will not be thwarted. Mordecai encourages Esther that she may be the instrument to achieve these purposes; he acknowledges the risk, but outlines how God's glory is worth it without using those exact words.

Esther's response in verses 15–17 is to go assemble all the Jews who were found in Susa for a three-day fast, which for the Jews is accompanied by prayer. She and her maidens will do the same, and then she, in her final statement of chapter 4, commits herself to the providential hand of her Creator by saying, "And thus I will go in to the king, which is not according to the law; and if I perish, I perish." Mordecai goes away and does what she says.

LIVING A LIFE SUBMITTED TO THE PROVIDENTIAL HAND OF GOD

Esther was human, like all of us. She had fears and dreams, hopes and aspirations. When faced with a crisis bigger than she could have ever imagined, her initial response was to retreat. However, in hearing the truth of God from Mordecai, courage came forth from this woman after God's own heart. She resolved to live her life under the providential hand of her loving Creator. She entrusted God with the results, all the while petitioning him in prayer for mercy on her behalf. We are not planted where we are by accident. We live where we live, work where we work, and are in the season we are in per the providential working of God. What is required of God's people where we are found is faithfulness that is rooted in absolute trust in the promises of God, fulfilled in the LORD Jesus, our Messiah and King. As a born-again believer in Jesus, you live to be a faithful follower of his, to share his word, to be an ambassador of his grace in both your acts of service and proclamation of the gospel to all you come into contact with, regardless of the costs. In Matthew 5:14, Jesus states, "You are the light of the world. A city set on a hill cannot be hidden; nor does anyone light a lamp and put it under a basket, but on the lampstand, and it gives light to all who are in the house. Let your light shine before men in such a way that they may see your good works, and glorify your Father who is in heaven." As followers of Jesus, we are saved for a time such as this. We are to daily submit to God's providence and be faithful to shine the light of Jesus in our actions and words to all with whom we live, for the goal is to bring glory to God the Father in the person of the LORD Jesus Christ. The only way we can truly live such a life is if, like Esther before us, we resolve by God's Spirit to "go in to the king, which is not according to the law; and if I perish, I perish."

William Borden was born in 1887 in Chicago. He was to be the heir of the Borden family dairy fortune. A life of ease and success was before him. However, after he graduated from high school, his father wanted William to see the world and, with a servant, some money, and a new Bible, sent him around the world. He traveled across Africa, Asia, and the Middle East. William saw a world of pain and suffering. He later wrote home, telling his father that instead of pursuing the family business, he intended to give his life to the hurting people of the world in missionary service. He knew the pain and hurt that would await him in such a calling, and as he reflected on that reality, he wrote the words "No Reserves" in his new Bible. He enrolled at Yale, where he ministered to the poor and the marginalized. Upon his graduation, offers to work on Wall Street flooded in, as well as the opportunity to come back to the family business or to go to law school. Rather, Borden chose to head to seminary and, upon his acceptance into seminary, he wrote in that same Bible his father had given him these words: "No Retreats." After graduating from Yale, he accepted a mission assignment to China. He stopped in Egypt in his transit to China and became ill and, at twenty-five years old, died. Before he had died, on his deathbed he had written in a now well-worn Bible the words "No Regrets."[14] William Borden lived a life dedicated wholly to the LORD Jesus' fame, and with no regrets surrendered to the providential hand of God over all things, even if it meant that he perished in this life. No reserves, no retreats, and no regrets can only be uttered by a life that embraces and lives in the reality that God reigns. Is that the reality where you find yourself dwelling each day?

DISCUSSION QUESTIONS

1. Who is Haman, and why does he hate Mordecai and the Jews?

14. Federer, *Great Quotations*, "Quote of John Ashcroft."

2. Why did Haman cast lots to determine the date of his plot to exterminate the Jews?

3. How do we see God's providential hand in the date selected by Haman, as well as all the details of Esther 3–4?

4. What do Mordecai and Esther's responses to the edict of Haman say about their faith or lack thereof?

5. How did Mordecai trust in God's sovereignty in his declaration to Esther?

3

The Puzzle Pieces Begin to Take Shape (Esther 5–6)

ON JANUARY 9, 2017, my brother, Jacob, passed away. He was twenty-six years old, and I was faced with the dauting and terrible task of officiating his funeral. Jacob was the youngest sibling in my family, and there were six years of difference in our ages. Growing up, I took him everywhere with me and in many ways, in light of our family situation, I helped raise him. He had one of the wittiest and most charismatic personalities of anyone I have ever known. He could make you laugh harder than you thought was possible. One of my favorite memories with him, as we competed over everything as he got older, was every time we could we found a mini-golf course to play. Throughout the course, much trash talk was exchanged, as well as bets made concerning what the loser would have to do in the event of their loss. Yes, I'm a Baptist, and yes, I made wagers with my brother. Most families hunt, hike, or fish. Jacob and I played mini golf and regular golf. After every game of mini golf, the winner would always keep the card and, for the next few days, they would find creative ways to rub in the victory they had the joy of experiencing in the face of the other brother's failure. Jacob was by far more creative in his conveyance of victory. I remember one morning waking up to the golf card, with his score and mine circled, taped to the ceiling. He felt that it was right and in good taste that I should wake up with the first thing being a reminder of his victory. Jacob was a larger-than-life personality and a wonderful brother. I loved him like a son. In many ways, he was my son. On January 9, 2017, I got the most unimaginable call. Jacob was dead. I remember that moment with extraordinary clarity as I struggled to process the reality that my beloved brother whom I adore was gone. He was dead. In the days that ensued, I wrestled with God and the word wondering "Why?" What good could come out of this? How does this puzzle piece make any sense at all? Well, I knew the theological answers, such as that we live in a fallen world, and I realized that. I realized that we all will die. I just didn't understand why Jacob had to go at twenty-six years old.

It was in those moments that the reality of God's character became an overwhelming source of comfort. God sovereignly reigns over all of life, and he is good even when I do not understand his secret counsels. It became a blanket over my torn soul to continually think on the truth that God did not take a pass on suffering. Jesus experienced more suffering in his endurance of God's infinite wrath for his people than I can ever attempt to imagine. In my grief and confusion, the reality of God's faithfulness, his character, and his sovereignty stilled the anxiety that threatened to consume my very soul. The puzzle pieces of life can often appear frightfully chaotic, and can be painful in crippling ways. However, as we continue to examine Esther, we will discover that it is in the difficult puzzle pieces that God's goodness is ultimately seen to God's eternal glory.

GOD DELIGHTS IN BEING A GREAT DELIVERER

The Old Testament gives us picture after picture of God as the Great Deliverer of his people. The New Testament culminates with Jesus Christ, who delivers us from our sin with great finality. God as the Great Deliverer is one of the most important threads you

THE PUZZLE PIECES BEGIN TO TAKE SHAPE (ESTHER 5-6)

will find through Scripture. If you asked a Jewish person in Esther's day what was the major act of God's deliverance of his people in history, the answer you would get unequivocally would be the exodus of God's people from Egypt to the promised land in Canaan. Psalms were written for God's people to reflect on this event (Pss 114; 136; etc.).

The deliverance of God's people out of oppression and bondage through God's miraculous intervention displayed God's power over nations. In this text, God's providential rule over all details of existence is highlighted as he delivers his people by moving kings and queens to achieve his decreed ends. The section of Scripture where we are highlights God as the Great Deliverer of his people, though he does it through his providential rule over mankind, rather than his miraculous intervention through signs and wonders like in the Exodus.

DO NOT LOOK FOR GOD IN THE WRONG PLACES

Unfortunately the miraculous, not the providential, is what many people seem to gravitate toward in the various circles of the Christian world when both are displays of God's great glory. The result is that people are often looking for a word from God in all the wrong places. I remember a family vacation when my oldest daughter was very young. My wife and I were out on a date while my sister-in-law was kind enough to watch my daughter for us. Now my daughter loves Cheez-Its, and she saw some on the dresser. While my daughter was sitting there talking to my sister-in-law, she pointed to the dresser and said, "Jesus." That's what my sister-in-law thought she said, anyway. My daughter just kept saying "Jesus, Jesus" over and over again. My sister-in-law began to wonder if Jesus was manifesting himself in the room. She started looking around thinking, is Jesus in the room? She even decided to give Jesus a greeting. However, she first began to listen more closely, and then understood that my daughter was not saying "Jesus" at all. Rather she was pointing to what was on top of the dresser and calling out for the Cheez-Its. Often, we think things that happen are signs from Jesus and, in reality, they are more "Cheez-Its" than anything else. Too often, God's people look at life by seeking signs based on our perceptions and feelings not submitted to Scriptural truth. Some are always looking for signs in situations, and we forget that Holy Scripture (the only specific revelation of God) has revealed that God is at work in the natural course of history and providentially leading it to its decreed conclusion. What we need to know is that the Holy Scripture as the word of God is what shapes and informs our minds so that we may discern what is right and pure and true (Rom 12:2). God rules over all details of human existence. All of them. God is fully everywhere all the time. Was Jesus in that room in his deity? Yeah. Did she see him? No. But Christ is fully everywhere all the time. He is guiding history, and he accomplishes his purposes in everyday life. There is nothing so minute that God does not care about and nothing too big that he does not reign over. The book of Esther proclaims that to us. God is working in all things for his everlasting glory, which perfectly coincides with the eternal good of his people.

ESTHER 5–6: IT WILL WORK OUT (THE PUZZLE COMES TOGETHER)

Esther 1–4 was all about God putting the pieces of his providential redemption of his people in their proper places. God raised up Esther, making her queen through the actions of Xerxes through him getting rid of Queen Vashti because she would not parade herself before a bunch of drunk men. Xerxes deposes her, and an empire-wide beauty pageant of sorts is held to find her replacement. Esther wins and is made queen in Vashti's place. Esther 3–4 reveals the enemy of the Jewish people who is going to seek their destruction. Haman and his rise to power is communicated by the author of the book of Esther as Haman becomes the second-highest official in the Persian kingdom. Haman is an Amalekite, a sworn enemy of the Jews, and he rises to a position of immense influence and power. Sparked by Mordecai's refusal to bow, Haman seeks vengeance against the entire Jewish people and manipulates Xerxes to sign an irrevocable decree to wipe the Jews out in the thirteenth day of the twelfth month. Mordecai, Esther's cousin who raised her, encourages Esther to go to the king and plead with him on behalf of her people. She originally says no because she does not want to die. However, Mordecai surmises that God may have put her in her royal position for a reason: "Who knows whether you have come and ascended to the kingdom for a time such as this?" Esther is heavily encouraged by Mordecai to go to the king and petition for the Jews. Before she goes, she has them fast for her. Beginning in Esther 5, the providential care of God for his people begins to be seen more clearly as the salvation of the Jews from extinction unfolds.

Esther 5 immediately picks up with Esther going to see the king, an act that would cost her everything if she should be received poorly by the king. Verses 1-2 state the following:

> Now it came about on the third day that Esther put on her royal robes and stood in the inner court of the king's palace in front of the king's rooms, and the king was sitting on his royal throne in the throne room, opposite the entrance to the palace. When the king saw Esther the queen standing in the court, she obtained favor in his sight; and the king extended to Esther the golden scepter which was in his hand. So Esther came near and touched the top of the scepter.

On the third day, Esther enters into the king's palace in front of the king's rooms and beholds the king sitting on the throne. Their eyes meet as he looks upon his queen standing in the court. Imagine that stressful moment, and then the joy of seeing the king extend his golden scepter. Esther is safely escorted to him, instead of to her death, and she comes near and touches the scepter as a sign of respect and submission. The king extends his scepter, for as verse 2 said, "she obtained favor in his sight." He sees her beauty and possibly remembers what struck him when he chose her as his queen. His heart is captured by her beauty, and he called her forth. After she approaches him, he dialogues with her, concerned and smitten. He asks her, "What is troubling you, Queen Esther?

And what is your request? Even to half of the kingdom it shall be given to you." He tells her that he will give her what she wants "up to half the kingdom," which was typical royal hyperbole for saying that he will grant her request, for he favors her. Esther responds in verse 4, "If it pleases the king, may the king and Haman come this day to the banquet that I have prepared for him." She lays her request before him and begins the process by which she will reveal to Xerxes her identity as a Jew and Haman's plot, with the hope that the king will deliver her people.

THE KING'S RESPONSE AND THE FIRST BANQUET

Xerxes's response is immediate and swift, and Esther's plan is precise. Esther 5:5–8 says this:

> Then the king said, "Bring Haman quickly that we may do as Esther desires." So the king and Haman came to the banquet which Esther had prepared. As they drank their wine at the banquet, the king said to Esther, "What is your petition, for it shall be granted to you. And what is your request? Even to half of the kingdom it shall be done." So Esther replied, "My petition and my request is: if I have found favor in the sight of the king, and if it pleases the king to grant my petition and do what I request, may the king and Haman come to the banquet which I will prepare for them, and tomorrow I will do as the king says."

Before we examine what has just transpired, let us take a moment to remember how the Persians made decisions. Persian monarchs, as seen in the book of Esther, are often intoxicated before deciding issues. The Persian monarchy, kings, and governors make important decisions in this book when they have had a ton of wine and they are intoxicated. Esther seems to be following that protocol, which is why she invited Xerxes and his chief governor, Haman, to a banquet. She is putting the two men in the same room together during a banquet in order to draw out Haman's plot before her husband. Here in verse 6, the king has had his fill of wine at the banquet that he and Haman were invited to. As the king drinks his wine, enjoying himself immensely, he looks at his beloved queen and asks, "What is your petition? For it shall be granted to you. What is your request? Even to the half of the kingdom it shall be done." Esther does not want half the kingdom (remember, this an idiom to indicate the king's favor); she just wants her life and the lives of her people spared. In verse 7, Esther gives what seems to be a strange reply. The king wants to grant her request. Here is Esther's opportunity to ask her husband to spare her people and to expose Haman. However, she responds along the lines of "may you, Haman, and I have a banquet tomorrow, and then I'll give you my request." This looks odd, almost as if she shirks the opportunity to reveal to Xerxes the plot and plead his favor, possibly out of fear. However, she lives in a time period when the customs are often very different than our own. Esther is following Ancient Near Eastern protocol. One commentator put it this way: "Esther was following typical Near Eastern protocol for presenting a request. She begins by asking for a small favor, but eventually she works her way, one concession at a time, to the real issue at hand. The banquet was a suitable setting for the requests to be made, for the Greeks observed that the Persians made their most important decisions while drunk."[1] She is buttering Xerxes up, and is doing it precisely per the protocol of her time.

The profound truth of Scripture glimmering through the cracks of human depravity is that God is providentially putting together the puzzle pieces of human actions (even sinful ones) to present his masterpiece of the Jews' salvation from utter ruin. What happens next is a stark display of irony regarding Haman's demise, but also a reminder that God rules over the hearts, minds, and willful decisions of mankind to bring all things to God's decreed end. In verses 9–14, Haman goes home joyful and elated, for he believes he has been honored greatly, having reached the pinnacle of success in his career. However, on the way home, Haman saw Mordecai at the gate, and Mordecai neither trembled or bowed before him. Haman, filled with pride and rage, restrains himself

---

1. Tomasino, "Esther," 494.

(verse 10) and goes home calling on all his family and friends to meet with him. At their arrival, Haman boasts of all his wealth, his promotions, and his position (verse 11). He then conveys the greatest honor he has beheld to date, which is being invited that to feast and drink wine privately with the king and queen (verse 12). This is the pinnacle of Haman's life, and the very next day will be his fall. He is having a big self-promotion party that would cause many politicians to blush. Haman recounted to his friends and his wife the glory of his riches and the number of his sons. The Persians considered having many sons to be very manly and influential.[2] As a matter of fact, every year the king would send the man with the most sons a special gift.[3] Haman also boasts of his authority in Xerxes kingdom.

Haman is exalting himself above all he knows. He is the epitome of human pride and will face the humiliation of divine wrath in a matter of hours, though his prideful heart thinks that it is not even in the realm of possibility. Despite all his perceived success, he is in agony because of Mordecai. He does not want to wait months before Mordecai is destroyed. He tells his wife Zeresh as much in verse 13. In verse 14, Zeresh tells him, "Have a gallows fifty cubits high made and in the morning ask the king to have Mordecai hanged on it; then go joyfully with the king to the banquet." Haman is pleased by this advice and immediately orders a gallows to be constructed. Haman is at the height of his hubris in this text, and the irony of his construction of the gallows will be conveyed in the coming chapters of Esther, for his demise will be by the very gallows he has built.

HAMAN IS A PICTURE OF FALLEN MAN

Haman here represents the state of every human being before God apart from God's grace. We are self-exalting rebellious creatures, as evidenced in multiple passages of Scripture: from wanting to be

2. Tomasino, "Esther," 494.
3. Tomasino, "Esther," 494.

our own gods in Genesis 3, to building a tower for our own glory in Genesis 11, to men gnashing their teeth at God in pride instead of repenting of sin in Revelation 16:10–11. This is mankind's natural disposition toward God: utter rebellion and self-exalting pride.

One of the greatest illustrations in all of Scripture concerning what God thinks about mankind in our rebellion is found in 2 Samuel 6 as David takes the ark back toward Jerusalem on a cart being pulled by oxen. The oxen stumbled, and the ark slid forward toward the dirt. Uzzah reached out his hand to steady the ark and God struck him down immediately for touching it. Why? This seems so harsh a move on God's part. The ark represented God's presence with the people. In steadying the ark with his hand, Uzzah made the fatal assumption that his hand was less offensive to God than the dirt the ark would fall upon. The human hand, as well as our whole being, does not do what it was originally designed to do, but dirt does. In this instance of Uzzah touching the ark, we see how God really looks upon us all apart from his grace in Jesus. We were beautifully created in the image of God in Genesis 1:27, but now we are ruined rebels who, apart from God's grace, deserve to be smitten from the earth at any moment. Unless God's grace brings us to repentance and faith, we will face his wrath, just as Haman will in Esther's story. Haman's pride precedes his judgment and everlasting ruin.

GOD TURNS THE HEART OF THE KING WHEREVER HE WISHES

"The king's heart is like channels of water in the hand of the LORD; He turns it wherever He wishes" (Prov 21:1). The very night Haman was boasting in his wealth, Xerxes was tossing in his bed, unable to find any rest. "During that night the king could not sleep so he gave an order to bring the book of records, the chronicles, and they were read before the king" (Esth 6:1). Without directly saying it, the author is implying how God's providential will is keeping the king from sleeping. While unable to sleep, the king calls for the book of memorable deeds to be read to pass the time. Now the form of the verb "read" in verse 1 of Esther 6 implies continuous and exhaustive reading, rather than a short review of the records.[4] In his restlessness, Xerxes stumbles upon the time when Mordecai had informed the king concerning a plot against the throne, and the king asked those who attended him what had been done to honor such a loyal deed. The young servant reading to him replied in verse 3, "Nothing has been done for him." The events behind this deed, if you recall, are recorded earlier in the book:

> In those days, while Mordecai was sitting at the king's gate, Bigthan and Teresh, two of the king's officials from those who guarded the door, became angry and sought to lay hands on King Ahasuerus. But the plot became known to Mordecai and he told Queen Esther, and Esther informed the king in Mordecai's name. Now when the plot was investigated and found to be so, they were both hanged on a gallows; and it was written in the book of the Chronicles in the king's presence. (Esth 2:21–23)

God's providential working, which made no sense earlier concerning its relevance to this story, now makes perfect sense. At the time he reported the assassination attempt, Mordecai had to wonder why his good deed was overlooked, especially considering the reality that Persian kings delighted in abundantly rewarding those who had distinguished themselves in their service to the king and kingdom.[5] God's divine rule over the events and affairs of kingdoms (countries today included) is meant to be seen clearly here. An act of excellent service toward the king just happened to be overlooked by a Persian king (a rare thing), and the night before Haman unveils his plot to kill Mordecai, the king reads of Mordecai's great deed. The Persians kept particular records, and the king then reflected on what to do to honor Mordecai, who so long ago protected and preserved the king and the kingdom by exposing a plot. Do you see the point the author is making without ever mentioning God's name? God works in the details, even ones that seemingly go unnoticed in order to accomplish his will. Think of

---

4. Tomasino, "Esther," 494.

5. Tomasino, "Esther," 494–95.

the timing of everything in this. Esther follows an oriental custom by not revealing the plot of Haman to her husband right away. She delays it one day, and the night before the next banquet Xerxes cannot sleep, so he has the book of deeds read to him, perhaps to help him sleep. He is reminded of what Mordecai has done for him and the kingdom; meanwhile, Haman is scheming to hang Mordecai on the same night that the king learns of Mordecai's service to the kingdom.

The king determines that something had to be done about this in verses 3-4 and asked his servants if there is anyone in the court. Haman strolls in with great excitement to propose the execution of Mordecai to Xerxes. The servants inform the king that his chief official is there, and Xerxes calls Haman into his presence in verse 5. Haman comes before Xerxes, but before Haman can utter the slightest word, the king asks him, "What should be done for the man whom the king desires to honor?" What do you think Haman is thinking at this point? The rest of verse 6 tells us that he assumes there is no one the king wishes to honor more than him. He is the king's top official. He was invited to a private banquet with the king and queen the previous day. He thinks that the king wants to honor him, and that idea influences his response to the king. Haman responds with how he wants to be honored:

> For the man whom the king desires to honor, let them bring a royal robe which the king has worn, and the horse on which the king has ridden, and on whose head a royal crown has been placed; and let the robe and the horse be handed over to one of the king's most noble princes and let them array the man whom the king desires to honor and lead him on horseback through the city square, and proclaim before him, "Thus it shall be done to the man whom the king desires to honor." (Esth 6:7b-9)

Robes are one of the most frequent gifts by the Persian kings, and the king's robes were unique.[6] Everyone in Susa would recognize the robe of the king. In addition, riding the king's horse would be a sign of royal favor, and the crown would signify the

---

6. Tomasino, "Esther," 495.

importance of the person riding the horse.[7] Haman has wealth, influence, and power already. What he wants is greater recognition from the people of Persia. He craves respect and fame, which is why he wants the king's most noble official (outside of himself) to lead the horse and proclaim Haman's favor to the people. Most people would have asked for money or a reward of sorts. Haman has enough money, and he wants to be exalted. His pride is beaming through his advice to the king.

Imagine being Haman who, at the moment, feels that all the world was in his hands. He came to have Mordecai, his archenemy, executed. Before he can speak, the king asks him for advice on how to honor someone. He thinks that he is the one to be honored, so he tells the king what he wants for himself. Xerxes responds with what must have been an anvil to Haman's pride, shattering his plans and purposes as well as his own idea of greatness in the Persian Empire: "Take quickly the robes and the horse as you have said, and do so for Mordecai the Jew, who is sitting at the king's gate; do not fall short in anything of all that you have said" (Esther 6:10).

Haman is undone. He obeys in verse 11 and then returns home to his wife in verse 13 with utter shame and humiliation. Zeresh, who once advised him to destroy Mordecai, now tells him that if Mordecai is a Jew, Haman is going to fall, which is a reference to the prophecies in Exodus 17:6 and Numbers 24:20.[8] Feel Haman's distress. He is unnerved, even anxious, and his wife sees the hand of the divine in all of this. Haman's plot to destroy the Jews is unraveling at a startling pace, and he who plotted the end of God's people is about to come to his own demise. As he mopes in despair, Haman is called to the second banquet with Xerxes and Esther in Esther 6:14, which sets up the deliverance of the Jews from Haman's plot in Esther 7–8.

7. Tomasino, "Esther," 495.
8. Tomasino, "Esther," 495.

THE PRINCIPLE OF PROVIDENCE

God's providential care over his people and his sovereignty over kings, circumstance, and all of life is now radiantly shining forth. The principle that God rules over all things cannot be emphasized in a more powerful way. The author is showing a real time in history where it seemed that all hope for God's people was gone, but now the rays of God's providence are brilliantly beaming forth to illuminate what was taking place in the darkness of human affairs.

This is not the first time where it seemed hopeless before God delivered his people. There are numerous examples from Scripture of God's deliverance of his people, through the splitting of the Red Sea all the way to the cross of Christ that redeems all God's people for all time. In Acts 4, Peter and John are let go from the ruling council of the Jews (the Sanhedrin) after having been incarcerated for preaching about Jesus after a miraculous healing in Jesus' name. They immediately go to the members of the early church and pray a very intriguing prayer. In this prayer they hold fast to God's providential care and make the following statement: "For truly in this city there were gathered together against Your holy servant Jesus, whom You anointed, both Herod and Pontius Pilate, along with the Gentiles and the peoples of Israel, to do whatever Your hand and Your purpose predestined to occur" (Acts 4:27–28). This statement presents the idea that Peter, John, and the church clung to the God who ruled over the choices of Pilate and the Jews in unjustly crucifying Jesus in order to accomplish the redemption of God's people forever. God sovereignly used the actions of evil men to glorify himself in the sacrifice of his Son, who endured the Father's wrath on his people's behalf, which magnified God's glory in justice satisfied and love eternally bestowed about his people. God rules over the decisions of men, and even in the darkest moments of life, where injustice seems to have won, God reigns. He is good. When nothing makes sense to us, this principle of God's providence should shower us with immovable hope and delight in God. If all we knew was Esther 1–5, we would have nothing but despair. Xerxes is a corrupt and cruel king. He is a drunkard and a savage. He campaigned in Greece and killed thousands of people. Haman hates the Jews and plots their execution, and Xerxes allows it. Does this make sense at all? No. Well, at least not yet. When you get to the end of Esther 6, it begins to make sense. We behold the providence of God and see why things are happening. We begin to understand that God is in control, even in the midst of our trials, pain, heartache, and hurt. Not only is he in control, but he works all things for his people's (those who trust in the LORD Jesus alone to save them from the penalty of their sin) good in Christ (Rom 8:28). The term "all things" means "all circumstances, situations, diseases, and events." The good that God is working for is our conformance to Christ, all to his glory. God cares for his church. He loves his redeemed people, and all the dire and darkness of this world are tools in his hand to bring about our eternal good, our everlasting joy in him.

GOD CARES FOR HIS PEOPLE

One of the greatest stories in all of Scripture that highlights God's providential care for his people, even in the minute details of life, is the book of Ruth, a story that takes place over six hundred years (approximately) earlier than Esther's time. Esther is all about delivering the Jews from annihilation, but Ruth is about God's care for a widow (Naomi) and her daughter-in-law (Ruth). Naomi and Ruth are women of no major consequence from a worldly perspective. They spend most of the narrative in Bethlehem, which is a little village in Judah. Naomi lost her husband and two sons while living in Moab, and Ruth the Moabite loves her mother-in-law and wants to stay with her, despite the death of her husband. Naomi and her family were originally from Bethlehem, but moved to Moab because of a severe famine, which was in contrast to God's revealed will in Scripture. They left the promised land for a pagan country. However, God's providential care is seen in how Naomi goes home to Bethlehem in Ruth 1.

Then, in Ruth 2–4, God provides for Ruth and Naomi's physical needs as well as their long-term security through a near relative,

Boaz, who will marry the widowed Ruth. What seems like chance, with Ruth gathering scraps of grain in Boaz's field, is God's providential care in all circumstances for Naomi and Ruth, including providing a child for Naomi's lineage to continue per Jewish custom; this child's descendants will include King David and, more importantly, King Jesus. God cares about the details of his people's life. He works all things for his redeemed people's good. Do you believe this? Do you believe that God reigns over everything in the universe? Do you believe he reigns over the evil actions and horrific circumstances of this world? Do not get me wrong—we cannot state that God is responsible for evil. However, it is clear that he has decreed to use the evil actions of fallen humanity to accomplish his will. The story of Ruth reminds us of God's providence over the small details, and the story of Esther reminds us of his providence over the large aspects of a people's existence.

There is something else behind Haman's actions that we also need to note, especially in light of the dualistic worldview of many professing Christians. God rules, not only over fallen mankind and our choices (as we see in the life of Haman), but also over fallen angels and their leader, Satan. As Paul says in Ephesians 6:11–12, "Put on the full armor of God, so that you will be able to stand firm against the schemes of the devil. For our struggle is not against flesh and blood, but against the rulers, against the powers, against the world forces of this darkness, against the spiritual forces of wickedness in the heavenly places."

GOD PROVIDENTIALLY RULES OVER SATAN

One of the most frustrating things to encounter as a pastor is to hear people talk about Satan as if he is equal with God in power and influence. I remember hearing a person say that both God and Satan want us; therefore, it is our job to choose between the two. Not only does this give Satan more power than he has, but it is blasphemous in that it puts the choice of good and evil within the will of man, when Scripture clearly shows that our will is unable to choose good apart from God's grace (Rom 3:9–23; Eph 2:1–4). The reality of Scripture is that God reigns over Satan. Satan can only do what God allows him to do. As a matter of fact, God uses what Satan does to ultimately achieve what God has decreed for his glory and the good of his people eternally. Let us look at a sample of Scriptures to see this truth.

Book of Job

In Job 1, all the angelic host appears before God's throne. Satan, a created and fallen angel, also reports to God. God mentions the faithful Job to Satan, who challenges God, saying that Job is only faithful because of God's blessing in Job's life. Satan carefully yet combatively speaks to God, saying that he cannot touch Job because God has protection around his faithful servant. It is clear that God reigns, and Satan is under that reign. Dualism dies in light of this text of Scripture. God permits Satan to afflict Job, but sets parameters of that affliction that Satan cannot cross (Job 1:12). Satan leaves, and freely does terrible things to Job's family and financial well-being. God providentially allows it, though Satan is responsible for the actions carried out. Satan is an instrument in God's hands. He is a lion, but he is on a leash and cannot go beyond the limits God has set. Throughout the affliction, God providentially brings Job to the place at the end of the book where Job sees God's glory and cherishes God above all things. Job never knows why he suffers, but if you read carefully, Job 42:1–6 makes clear that Job comes to a place where he resolutely trusts in God, for God's glory is more beautiful to him than all the family and possession that was taken away. God used Satan's affliction to produce Christlike character in Job.

1 Samuel 15:14–23

In 1 Samuel 15:14–23, Saul had the right to the throne of Israel taken from him, though he remained king for many years after his disobedience to God in 1 Samuel 14. God punishes Saul by sending an evil spirit in verse 14 to terrorize him, perhaps to bring him to repentance or to seal his judgment. Either way, what is clear is that God sends the evil spirit. The evil spirit is used by God to accomplish God's will in Saul, sending for a skilled musician named David to play when Saul was afflicted. Earlier in 1 Samuel 15, David was anointed to be the next king of Israel, and due to God's providential reign over even those angels in rebellion against him, he is allowed to observe the court and kingship of Saul in preparation for his coming kingship.

1 Chronicles 21:1 and 2 Samuel 24:1

In 1 Chronicles 21:1 the author conveyed that Satan stood against Israel and David to move David to take an unlawful and prideful census, which brought God's judgment. In 2 Samuel 24:1, the author explains the event by citing the LORD God as the one who incited David to take a census in order to bring due judgment to Israel and humble David's pride. How can both God and Satan be behind the same event? The solution is simple. God sovereignly allowed David to be tempted by Satan, which then brought the disobedience and judgment of David and the nations. God used Satan's actions to accomplish his good purposes, humbling David and judging Israel for their sin.

2 Chronicles 18:18-22

In 2 Chronicles 18:18-22, God is seen on his heavenly throne and asks for a spirit to entice King Ahab to go to defeat in battle. A fallen angel volunteers to do it, and God sends the fallen angel to move false prophets to convey false things to Ahab so that Ahab will go into battle and die as punishment for his rebellion against God, despite God's continuous common grace to him during his evil rule. God reigns over all fallen angels, and though he is not responsible for their evil, he allows it and uses it for his good ends.

Matthew 4:10–11 and John 13:26–27

Jesus is tempted by Satan in Matthew 4:1–11, and at the end of that temptation commands Satan to leave. Satan obeys. God allows Satan to tempt Jesus to display Jesus as the perfect Son, in contrast to Israel, the sinful son. The interesting part of this text is that Jesus is able to command Satan. Satan is on a leash, and the Triune God (God the Father, God the Son, God the Holy Spirit) controls it. In John 13:26–27, Satan enters into Judas, and after that Jesus commands Judas and Satan to do what they have plotted. Jesus uses Satan and Judas to achieve the ends of his crucifixion through the betrayal of Judas. Jesus was not some helpless victim. He was sovereign over all events, including his passion on the cross. Jesus rules over Satan. Jesus allows Satan to do certain things in order to achieve the Triune God's will. Jesus even allows Satan to blind the hearts of people who will not believe in him to the truth, in order to achieve the LORD's judgment against mankind, who rejects him (2 Cor 4:3–4).

Luke 22:31–34 and Revelation 13:7

Luke 22:31–34 is a dialogue with Jesus and Peter wherein Jesus tells Peter that Satan has demanded permission to sift him as wheat. Jesus prayed for Peter, and ensured him that he would return to Jesus, calling Peter to strengthen the church. In Revelation 13:7, we see that Satan is permitted to make war on followers of Christ for a season and to bring the peoples of the world under his evil sway. Why? Per various Scripture, I believe it is to display God's glory in the way that his people endure and overcome in the LORD Jesus, and how they treasure him above life itself (1 John 5:4–5; John 12:25; Rom 8:36–37; Rev 2:26). Satan and his fallen angels are unwittingly used by God for God's purposes. God reigns.

GOD REIGNS

God reigns over the spiritual and physical realms. He providentially uses the free actions of spiritual beings as well as the actions of human beings to accomplish his good purposes, determined before time began. The reason this should comfort us is that we will face hard days, as Esther and Mordecai did. We will need to confront times in our lives where all seems to have fallen apart, and we will want to yell, "the sky is falling!" However, in those moments, we know that God reigns, and that he is working for the good of his people to the glory of his name forever and ever.

At the beginning of this chapter, I described the death of my brother. It was in that time these truths became real. How could my God, who I know is good per the truth of Scripture, bring my brother to an early grave. To be honest, like Job, I do not completely know why to this day. However, through the process of grieving, as well as grappling with the word of God, I see more clearly than ever that I do not have to know why. I simply see the beauty and goodness of a God in Scripture who reigns over all things for the glory of his name and for the good of his people. My hope is found in nothing less than his beauty and his providential care over my heart and life. He is good. He reigns. Why worry? Rather, it is best to rest in him, even when the puzzle pieces are still coming together. In our next chapter, we will see his glory beam forth with unhindered clarity, which I pray provokes our awe of God.

DISCUSSION QUESTIONS:

1. How are the puzzle pieces in Esther coming together for God to deliver his people thus far?

2. How is Haman's pride reflected in our own lives?

3. Why does Esther approach the king the way she does?

4. How does the doctrine of God's sovereign providence give you boldness?

5. How does the doctrine of God's sovereign providence over the material and spiritual realm give you peace in your day-to-day life?

4

God's Providential Portrait of His Glory (Esther 7—9:19)

HAVE YOU EVER PONDERED why God does all that he does? Or perhaps you have asked questions such as "why am I here?" Many people spend their entire life looking for their purpose, when it is really quite simple. In its opening question and answer, the Westminster Catechism conveys the meaning of life. It states the following: (Q) "'What is the chief end of man?' (A) 'Man's chief end is to glorify God and to enjoy Him forever.'"[1] The chief end of man is to glorify God and enjoy him forever. A Christian's purpose is to magnify God's greatness in the LORD Jesus. The reason we are created to glorify God and enjoy him forever is that God does all things for his glory and the enjoyment of himself as the greatest of all beings. If God does otherwise, he would be an idolater, and not God. God does all things for his glory. God redeems his people for his glory. God is benevolent to the world for his glory. God is just and righteous against rebellion for his glory. God is love, which is seen in his treatment of his people, for his glory. In Isaiah 48:9, God tells Israel, "For the sake of My name I delay My wrath,

---

1. Cross and Livingstone, *Oxford Dictionary*, 1745.

And for My praise I restrain it for you, in order not to cut you off." God follows this statement up with "And My glory I will not give to another" at the end of verse 11. God's glory and the good of his people are not at odds. Remember from the last chapter the truth of Romans 8:28: "And we know that God causes all things to work together for good to those who love God, to those who are called according to His purpose." God gets much glory as he works for his redeemed people's good, which is learning to enjoy and savor him above all. God delights in redeeming his people so that they may savor him and his glory and enjoy him forever. Psalms 37:4 tells us that we are to delight in the LORD, and he will give us the desires of our heart (which reflect his own heart more when we delight in him). God's glory, revealed in the salvation of his people in the book of Esther, portrays him as the Good Deliverer of his people. These truths are meant to move our minds and hearts to delight in such a God who reigns over the cosmos and delights to deliver his people from destruction.

WHY IS THIS SO IMPORTANT?

Why is it so important for us to see God's glory in the deliverance of his people in the past and see the Scriptural declaration of our ultimate deliverance (glorification) in the future? It is because we all face trials and tribulations. At the church where I pastor, we hand out study Bibles to newly-baptized followers of Jesus. In those Bibles, I usually write Acts 14:22 underneath the date of their baptism in the front of the Bible. In Acts 14:22, Paul tells the churches he saw planted in his first missionary journey, "through many trials and tribulations we must enter the kingdom of God." The reason the glory of God in salvation is so important is that we will face trials and tribulations. Only a robust view of God from Scripture will see us through to the end. The problem with much of evangelicalism today is we have become man-centered. We present God as bowing to the will of man, instead of man submitting to the will of God. The church today more or less views God like he is this puny beggar in heaven instead of the providential

King of the universe who rules all things, whose plans man cannot thwart. It was evident, in our last election cycle, through the constant social media feeds and posts by Christians, that the perceived idea of a "Great America" mattered more to many than the gospel. Many professing Christians resorted to a barrage of constant status updates and Twitter posts with unloving political punchlines, as well as name-calling and character assassination of all who disagreed with them. Jesus said in Luke 6:45 that out of the heart the mouth speaks. Do not misunderstand me: biblically, we are to be great citizens and pray, as well as work for the good of our country (Rom 13:1–7; Jer 29:7). However, most were approaching the election with a mindset that, if we did not go a certain way, we were doomed, and the country we have known would fall apart. So many Christians displayed a lack of trust in the sovereignty of God. Again, do not misread what I'm saying. We should study the issues as informed citizens, pray diligently, vote well, and strive to be excellent citizens, salt and light in our communities. Most importantly, we as God's people are not to be frantically terrified at every cultural storm in our world. We are to be bold—yet loving—in truth, and restful in the providence of God over all nations, including our own.

Sadly, the church often acts like God is not in control, which is evidenced in our constant complaining. Instead, we should be consistently sharing the gospel and performing acts of goodness in our communities. The book of Esther reminds us of this and compels us to see God, who reigns over nations and wicked rulers to accomplish his purposes for his glory. If God is all-powerful and if he is providently directing all things, what do you and I need to fear if we are his sojourning people? Esther 7—9:19 helps us to savor the answer to that question. For God delights, in his glory, to deliver his people.

ESTHER 7–8: HAMAN'S END AND THE JEWS' DELIVERANCE

Remember what has transpired up to this point. Haman had to honor Mordecai through the streets the very morning he planned to have him killed on the gallows. Haman is escorted at the end of Esther 6 to the second banquet with King Xerxes and Queen Esther. Esther 7 picks up with the events of that feast:

> Now the king and Haman came to drink wine with Esther the queen. And the king said to Esther on the second day also as they drank their wine at the banquet, "What is your petition, Queen Esther? It shall be granted you. And what is your request? Even to half of the kingdom it shall be done." Then Queen Esther replied, "If I have found favor in your sight, O king, and if it pleases the king, let my life be given me as my petition, and my people as my request; for we have been sold, I and my people, to be destroyed, to be killed and to be annihilated. Now if we had only been sold as slaves, men and women, I would have remained silent, for the trouble would not be commensurate with the annoyance to the king." Then King Ahasuerus asked Queen Esther, "Who is he, and where is he, who would presume to do thus?" Esther said, "A foe and an enemy is this wicked Haman!" Then Haman became terrified before the king and queen. (Esth 7:1–6)

Haman comes to the second banquet, and they are drinking per the Persian custom; after the king has had his fill of wine, he says to Esther, "What do you want? You have my favor up to half my kingdom." Esther's reply is bold. Though flawed, she is faithfully executing her task before God (and by his grace, which gives her strength) to ask for her people's deliverance. She responds to the king, essentially saying, "If I have found favor in your sight, O King, let my life be given me as a petition and my people as my request, for we have been given over to destruction, to be killed and annihilated. If we were only going to be slaves, I would not speak so in order to avoid annoying the king." Xerxes is shocked. His response shows that he is furious that anyone would dare to do harm to his queen. At this point, Haman has to be thinking, "Surely she is not a Jew."

Up to this point, we have seen that Xerxes is a hot-tempered mess. He responds with fury: "Who would dare threaten my queen?" In reality, Xerxes was the one who had done it when he gave the signet ring to Haman to approve his proposal. Haman is shaking in his proverbial boots as his whole plan is unraveling before his very eyes. Haman sees the king's rage. His doom is imminent, and he begins to sense it. Esther responds to the king's inquiry about who it is that has done this in verse 6, as she identifies Haman as the wicked person who had brought this about. The king stands up with rage in verse 7 and goes into the garden. Haman stays to beg for his life before Queen Esther. At the end of verse 7, Queen Esther is reclining on the couch next to the table and Haman falls at her feet, begging her for his life. The king walks back into the banquet in verse 8 after having collected himself. He sees Haman falling at the queen's feet, and it looks like Haman is assaulting her. An odd (and rather lucky) turn of events for the Jews, right? No, it is God's providence. Xerxes declares, "Will he even assault the queen with me in the house?" (Esth 7:8). The king orders a bag to be put over Haman's head, and he is taken to the very gallows that Haman had constructed for Mordecai's execution. They hang Haman on those gallows in verse 10, and then the king calms down.

Haman's house and wealth is given to Esther (Esth 8:1). Mordecai is then promoted (Esther has told the king who he is), and Esther sets Mordecai over Haman's household in verse 2. The signet ring given by the king to Mordecai probably signifies that Haman's position is now Mordecai's. Mordecai is given Haman's money, his property, his influence and now he is given his position as the second-highest ruler in the kingdom. The enemy of the Jews has been destroyed. However, the problem of his decree in the king's name remains. But before we move to that, it is important to see how so much has changed in a day. Haman was one of the wealthiest men in the empire the day before, but now he is dead, and his enemy Mordecai has his wealth. Mordecai's corpse was supposed to be hanging from the gallows, and that position has been occupied by Haman's.

God's Deliverance of His People from Destruction

The edict to destroy the Jews was still in effect. Remember, per Persian law, edicts of the king could not be revoked. Something had to be done. Esther appears before the king again without an invitation in Esther 8:3–4, and he brings her near. He loves her, or at least her beauty. Esther's request was simple (as seen in verses 5–6). She wanted a second decree composed and distributed throughout the empire to override the first one.[2] Esther identifies with her people and pleads for them. We see here in this passage Esther faithfully and courageously identifying with her people, pleading their cause before the king. Xerxes responds in verses 7–8 by reminding Mordecai and Esther that he has given them Haman's estate and Haman's authority. He commissions them to write a new edict to offset the first, because what the king has initially written cannot be overturned. Mordecai gathers the scribes of the kingdom and issues the following edict, described in Esther 8:11–12:

> In them the king granted the Jews who were in each and every city the right to assemble and to defend their lives, to destroy, to kill and to annihilate the entire army of any people or province which might attack them, including children and women, and to plunder their spoil, on one day in all the provinces of King Ahasuerus, the thirteenth day of the twelfth month (that is, the month of Adar).

Through Mordecai's new decree, the king granted the Jews everywhere in the empire the right to assemble, defend themselves, and plunder their enemies. The word "assemble" in the Hebrew means to gather arms, to form an army.[3] The Jews can defend themselves against the entire army of any people or province which might attack them on that one day. The same wording used by Haman in

2. Martin, "Esther," 708–13.
3. Tomasino, "Esther," 498.

his decree is used by Mordecai in his. The irony here is striking! God's power of the peoples of the world is portrayed here with great clarity. The edict goes out, and it is sent by the fastest horses in Persia per verse 14. In verse 15, Mordecai is promoted before the king, donning the royal robes of blue, as well as a large golden crown. He has become one of top officials in the Persian Empire, and his influence in the book of Esther will continue to grow. The message spreads quickly throughout Persia, and the people of Persia respond in fear, which leads to the profession of many to become part of the covenant people of God. In verse 17, pagans throughout Persia forsake idol worship as a result of God's glory, revealed in the salvation given to his people. The people of God have joy, gladness, and honor. So why do pagan Persians, worshipers of idols, forsake them and submit to the God of Abraham, Isaac, and Jacob? The answer is that they saw God's glory amongst his people and were drawn to trust in his promises.

GOD'S GLORY REVEALED IN HIS PEOPLE DRAWS PEOPLE UNTO HIM

Today, a lot of times, churches will draw people in through worldly means. They will take on worldly practices and even cater to seekers in order to see them profess faith in the promises of God fulfilled in Jesus. The method of God throughout Scripture and seen here in Esther is quite different. The people of God are regulated in their worship by the Scripture itself, and we should look drastically different from the world. What attracts people is the church's proclamation of the salvation wrought by Jesus to the praise of God. The world seeing the power of such a message in the joy, gladness, and transformed lives of God's people will draw others out of the dark world to such light. As I have heard it said in so many contexts, "what you win them with, you win them to." When the glory of God in the redemptive work of Jesus is treasured above all things, some people are drawn to it. Some people repel it. We see this in Acts 16 when Paul and Silas are imprisoned in Philippi on Paul's second missionary journey. In the heart of the prison, they are praying and singing hymns of praise to God. The prisoners are listening intently. A great earthquake hits, the prison doors are opened, and everyone's chains are unfastened. The jailer rushes in, knowing that if any prisoner is missing he will be required to take their punishment. He pulls out his sword in order to take his own life, and Paul cries out from the darkness, "Do not do it!" The jailer falls before Paul and asks him what he must do to be saved. Why would he do that? He must have heard the prayers they spoke and praises they sang, seeing the character of Christ's redemptive work in their lives. In short, the jailer saw God's glory in Jesus manifested through them, which drew him to the gospel that Paul and Silas preached.

When our lives, in bad circumstances or in favorable ones, show an unwavering delight in Jesus and a persevering faith in his finished work, people will take notice. When the evidence of God's deliverance is seen in our lives and heard from our lips, people will take notice. That is what happened when the Jews rejoiced at hearing of their deliverance from their enemies by their faithful God.

THE TRIUMPH OF THE JEWS BY GOD'S PROVIDENCE (ESTHER 9:1–19)

The Jews heard the proclamation of their deliverance in chapter 8, and in chapter 9 we see it come to fruition. The Jews assemble in their cities on the designated day and destroy their enemies. The officials of the Persian empire assist them because of their fear of Mordecai, who has risen in power to one of the king's most influential and powerful officials (Esth 9:3). Throughout the empire, the Jews destroy seventy-five thousand of those who tried to harm them and plunder them (verse 16). In Susa, they destroyed five hundred men on the first day, and then the king gave two orders: first, the Jews would be given another day to exact vengeance, exclusively in Susa. The result was that three hundred more were destroyed by the Jews on the fourteenth day (verses 11–15). Second, Haman's ten sons were to be hanged on the gallows there.

The Jews were not interested in plunder on either day, as noted in verses 10, 15, and 16. Unlike Saul, who took plunder when he was commanded not to when he conquered the Amalekites (1 Sam 15:9), the people of God in the book of Esther did not take plunder (and thereby repeat Saul's error). They simply defended their lives for the glory of God. They wanted no material gain, but merely desired to live and worship the LORD of Hosts. Their motive was not the temporal pursuit of wealth, but the eternal glory of God.

Now a question may have arisen in your mind: "How can this Persian king allow so many people to perish at the hands of the Jews?" Xerxes is indifferent toward the destruction of 75,800 of his own people. Many scholars have a hard time with this, but considering Xerxes's character, as demonstrated both in this book and in historical records, this is not something that should be surprising. Rather, it should be almost expected of a king who did not value human life as much as his own sensual pleasure. After the first execution of the enemies of the Jews, Xerxes is taken aback at hearing of the death toll in Susa. However, concerned as he may be about the death toll around the empire, he is even more concerned with pleasing his queen. This is shown in his statement to Queen Esther. He states, "Now what is your petition? It shall be granted you. And what is your further request? It shall also be done" (Esth 9:12). Esther uses this opportunity to further the defense of the Jews against their enemies, as previously discussed. Verses 17–19 explain how the Jews made the day after their deliverance (the fourteenth day of the month of Adar, February or March on our calendar) a day of rest and celebration. However, though the Jews outside Susa celebrated on the fourteenth day, the Jews in Susa celebrated on the fifteenth day a day of rest, because they had had an extra day to destroy their attackers. This celebration explains the practice of Purim being the fourteenth and fifteenth days of the month of Adar. The author uses all of this in order to communicate the reason behind the Jewish festival of Purim (which we will look at in chapter 5), a time the Jewish people celebrate with joy and giving every year.

GOD'S DELIVERANCE WAS IN THE DETAILS

This story is one of the greatest stories in Scripture of God mani-festing his power, love, and providential care in the salvation he worked on behalf of his people. The Jews were headed for destruc-tion, and now they have life and favor. The lineage by which the Messiah would come has been preserved. God's people have been delivered, and those in him have an unshakeable hope, even as they sojourn in a pagan empire. Unlike the parting of the Red Sea, where God delivered his people by parting the waters, in the book of Esther God chooses to deliver his people by using the actions of kings and peoples for his glory. Though the means for achieving the deliverance of the Jews was different than, for example, when God struck the Egyptians with ten plagues to free his people from bondage, the deliverance is no less amazing. God is seen to rule over all the minute details of existence to a such a degree that even those who oppose his revealed will (Scripture) shall ultimately unknowingly serve his sovereign will. By causing even those op-posing him to serve his sovereign will, he exalts his power and wisdom to all peoples. He demonstrates his love for his people in saving them from destruction.

THIS PRINCIPLE IS SEEN IN THE LIFE OF SAUL OF TARSUS

In Acts 1:8, right before his ascension to glory, Jesus tells his dis-ciples, "but you will receive power when the Holy Spirit has come upon you; and you shall be My witnesses both in Jerusalem, and in all Judea and Samaria, and even to the remotest part of the earth." The disciples go to Jerusalem and wait for the Holy Spirit, who em-powers Peter in Acts 2 to preach, with the result of three thousand people trusting in Jesus. In Acts 1–6, the gospel has gone through Jerusalem to Judea. Yet, per the LORD Jesus in Acts 1:8, the gos-pel was to go to Samaria and the ends of the earth as well. God chooses to spread the gospel to Samaria by the death of Stephen and the persecution of the church by Saul of Tarsus. Saul, a devout

Pharisee at the time, believes he is serving God by seeking out and imprisoning these people who follow a crucified messiah. Acts 8:3 describes Saul's activity as a ravaging of the church, going to home after home and dragging men and women into prison. The result in Acts 8:4 was that many scattered and took the gospel to the Samaritan region, where eventually many people repented and believed in Jesus. At the time it may not have been a thought in their minds that God would spread his gospel through persecution against the church. God's glory was displayed in his use of Saul of Tarsus's active rebellion against the revealed will of God to save an entire people, who had the gospel shared with them through those who fled persecution.

The reality is that God will accomplish his purposes in the world. Even those who oppose God, who stand against God's truth and moral standards, will be instruments in his hand to ultimately accomplish his sovereign will. God's plans cannot and will not be thwarted, and will always be accomplished. Proverbs 19:21 states, "Many plans are in a man's heart, But the counsel of the LORD will stand." God will achieve all his purposes to bring about the salvation of people from every tribe, tongue, and nation, who will magnify his glory forever while dwelling with him on the New Earth (Rev 7; 21–22).

HOW DOES THIS AFFECT ME?

I remember sitting down with an older and wiser pastor who must have seen that I needed counsel. I was twenty-eight and new in ministry, and I must confess that I was in over my head. Looking back, I had so much to learn about pastoring a church and still do by God's grace. This older pastor, seasoned from many years of shepherding the flock of God at our local church, was talking about preaching sermons early on that were theologically pointed and which would have impressed any seminary professor. However, they were not reaching into the hearts and affections of the people he was called to lovingly shepherd from the word of God. I remember him looking across the office room at me and making sure my eyes were locked to his when he said this with humble conviction: "Not only do we want to tell them from the word the truth of Scripture, but we are called to share with them how these truths affect each of us." The Bible is filled with timeless, unchanging truths, and these truths have many applications. What we need to ask ourselves at this moment is this: how do all the truths we have seen in the book of Esther up to this point affect each of us? In essence how does the truth of God's providential rule over history affect me? Here is a sample of a few ways.

God's providential sovereignty brings boldness

He has promised that a people from every tribe, tongue, and nation will know his salvation in Christ (Matt 24:14). He will use all actions, both good and evil, to achieve this end. In light of that, we can expend our lives in the service of his gospel, knowing no matter how severe and tough the trials, in the end God's word will not return void, and a people will come to Christ out of this world for God's glory. What moves faithful missionaries (such as William Carey, considered the father of modern-day missions) to endure the years of seemingly fruitless labor? It is the reality that God will save a people for himself from every tribe, tongue, and nation, and will even use adverse circumstances we face to ultimately bring that end. This is a comfort of immeasurable value in the valleys of life for all who live to proclaim the gospel to the nations for the LORD Jesus' fame amongst them.

God's providential sovereignty propels us to fervent prayer

Esther, Mordecai, and all the Jews in Susa fasted and sought God in prayer. God's response was to display his glory as the Great Giver of all good things to his people by delivering Esther and the Jews from destruction. In John 14:13–14, Jesus communicates to his disciples that whatever they ask in his name, he will do it in order that God the Father may be glorified. Asking in Jesus' name means approaching God the Father through Jesus and praying per the will of Jesus in the world. The promise here is profound. As we go to the Father through the Son (whose redemptive work gives us access to the Father), whatever we ask in accordance with God's will he delights to give us for the praise of his Name. God has ordained to display his glory in great ways by answering the prayers of his people (through the LORD Jesus) and using the way they fervently follow his will.

God's providential sovereignty comforts and calms our hearts

God is not a man that he should lie, nor does he change (Num 23:19; James 1:17). He was faithful to his people in the days of Esther, he is faithful today, and he will be faithful tomorrow. This truth in light of God's reign over all details of life allows us to calm our fears if we are followers of Christ, with the reality that God reigns and works for my good, even when it means temporary pain and suffering. This truth allows us to rest. In John 14:1, Jesus told his disciples to not let their heart be troubled and to believe in God and believe also in him. He reminded them that he and the Father rule over all things and he was in control of every event, including his betrayal by Judas and his impending crucifixion at the hands of the Jews and Romans. The sovereignty of God is the doctrine Jesus used to still the stormy waters of his disciples' anxious and fearful hearts.

The reality of this was cemented in my consciousness several years ago, as a member of the church where I pastor was getting his heart checked and was delivered dire news. In response to the doctor's diagnosis, this brother in Christ, with an undeniable and unshakeable confidence, beamed with joy, proclaiming that all was well, for God reigns and he is good. In the moment of this man's darkest hour, the light of God's love for his people and his sovereignty over all things was not just a source of comfort, but the source of his joy. Interestingly, this brother went to the doctor later, and as we sat in the office, the blockage that was to be fatal did not appear on the scans. The reality of Psalm 115:1-3 was seen in his life.

Psalms 115:1-3

> Not to us, O LORD, not to us, but to your name give glory, for the sake of your steadfast love and your faithfulness!
> Why should the nations say, "Where is their God?"
> Our God is in the heavens; he does all that he pleases.

God reigns, and he does everything that he pleases. The message of Esther shows this truth in every detail coming together for the Jews' deliverance from annihilation. The doctrine of God's providence and loving care for his people should empower us by his Spirit to live out the reality that, amidst a fallen world, we must stop worrying, for he reigns.

DISCUSSION QUESTIONS:

1. How is God glorified by redeeming his people from destruction?

2. What about God's deliverance of his people draws others to come to know him in faith?

3. Contrast and compare God's deliverance of the Jews here in Esther with the deliverance from Egypt. How do both bring him glory?

4. How does the truth of God's providential redemptive work seen in Esther move you to active obedience to the LORD Jesus as his disciple?

5. How does this truth change your prayer life and your perception of your problems?

5

Stop Worrying, He Reigns
(Esther 9:20—10:3)

HAVE YOU EVER FORGOTTEN an important event, birthday, or anniversary? Perhaps you, like me, often have a hard time remembering the location of your vehicle at the store parking lot. Most of us mere mortals have. As a matter of fact, the Scriptures show that God's people are characterized by forgetfulness. It is why, during many of our obstacles in life, we will complain at God, or lament that the sky seems to be falling around us. In perusing through the books of Exodus and Numbers, there is a singular frustration expressed toward Moses, the leader God appointed over Israel to bring them to the promised land and give them the law. At every difficulty, the people complained against him and Aaron, seemingly forgetting God's provision for them and the display of his wonders throughout their trip to Sinai. They repeatedly complained about the food, their lack of water, and even about their inability to conquer the promised land. For some perspective, this was a people who had seen the glory of God in the pillar of fire in the camp, who had manna from heaven in the morning and quail in the evening, six days a week. They had seen God cripple Egypt and part the

Red Sea so that they could pass through on dry land. However, in failing to reflect on the past providential faithfulness of God, they were constantly in a state of turmoil and anxiety, which produced constant complaining against God's current provision. God calls us to remember his works in the past to propel us to current faithfulness and worship, even in contrary circumstances.

The author of Psalms 111 presents the importance of remembering and thinking on the works of God. Let us look carefully at what the psalmist says concerning the works of God and their place in our thoughts.

> Praise the LORD!
> I will give thanks to the LORD with all my heart,
> In the company of the upright and in the assembly.
> *Great are the works of the LORD;*
> *They are studied by all who delight in them.*
> Splendid and majestic is His work,
> And His righteousness endures forever.
> *He has made His wonders to be remembered;*
> The LORD is gracious and compassionate.
> *He has given food to those who fear Him;*
> He will remember His covenant forever.
> *He has made known to His people the power of His works,*
> In giving them the heritage of the nations.
> *The works of His hands are truth and justice;*
> *All His precepts are sure.*
> They are upheld forever and ever;
> They are performed in truth and uprightness.
> He has sent redemption to His people;
> He has ordained His covenant forever;
> Holy and awesome is His name.
> *The fear of the LORD is the beginning of wisdom;*
> A good understanding have all those who do His commandments;
> His praise endures forever. (Ps 111; my emphases)

The psalmist is reflecting on God's works, revealed to God's people through God's word, and it is bringing him to praise God. When the people of God forget the works of God that display his glory, we end up in the same state as God's chosen people, wandering the wilderness in Exodus and Numbers. We become complainers, discontent and disillusioned. We are called to remember what God has done for his people. Esther 9:20—10:3 is a call to celebrate God's deliverance of the Jews from the destruction determined by Haman every year. The idea was to keep the people of God from forgetfulness and, amidst trying times, have reminders in place like Purim to reassure them of both God's rule over all events in history to their right end (providence) and his covenantal love for them that will not fail.

REMEMBER GOD'S PAST DELIVERANCE

In Esther 9:20, Mordecai records all the events concerning the deliverance of the Jews from destruction and sends letters to all the Jewish people throughout the Persian kingdom, binding them in verse 21 to celebrate God's deliverance from Haman's plot on the fourteenth and fifteenth days of the month of Adar. Per verse 22, they were to celebrate by giving gifts to the poor and sending food to one another, which the Jews put into practice in verse 23 at Mordecai's heeding. The author summarizes in verses 24–25 the events that had taken place and the reason for the celebration of the Jews. The author states,

> For Haman the son of Hammedatha, the Agagite, the adversary of all the Jews, had schemed against the Jews to destroy them and had cast Pur, that is the lot, to disturb them and destroy them. But when it came to the king's attention, he commanded by letter that his wicked scheme which he had devised against the Jews, should return on his own head and that he and his sons should be hanged on the gallows.

This summary gets at the heart of all that took place in the entire book, and yet the main character is the One who was guiding all these events for his glory, because his Name is connected to his people.

Purim: A Celebration of God's Deliverance

The author in verses 26–27 describes why the celebration and memorial is called Purim. Mordecai named it after the lot that Haman cast to determine the date of the Jews destruction. In Esther 3:7, the lot that was cast for Haman to determine when to seek the Jews destruction was called "Pur." The text outlines that the Jews' committed themselves to celebrate this two-day memorial each year at the appointed time in remembrance of the days the Jews throughout the empire rested from their enemies. Esther 9:28–32 brings this section to a conclusion, noting a powerful commission by the authority of Queen Esther to keep this holiday in remembrance of God's deliverance of his people. The author then moves into Esther 10:1–3, where Xerxes's power is presented in his ability to execute a tribute in all his lands, even in the coastlands, to his own accomplishments, as well as Mordecai's promotion. Mordecai's service for his people is also highlighted and remembered. It is an odd way to end the book, but profound when you realize that we see the silent message of the book: God rules over pagan kings, God uses the natural events of human history to achieve his decreed ends to display his fame.

Think about all that God has done once more. God raised a Jewish orphan to Queen in Persia. God took a man of the Jews, Mordecai, who was doomed to the gallows, all the way to the second-in-command in the Persian Empire, just as God had previously done in the life of Joseph. God even used pagan superstition like the casting of lots to set a date, whereby he would providentially secure all that needed to take place before that date came and went. God gave Queen Esther favor before Xerxes in the throne room. God prevented Xerxes from sleeping the night before Haman's proposed execution of Mordecai, and even moved him to look at the record of the empire, where Mordecai's deed was described. God used Esther's understanding of protocol to present Haman's folly in the perfect time, leading to Haman's own death on the gallows he had built for Mordecai. God reigns, and he calls his people to reflect on his works.

FORGETFULNESS PRECEDES FAITHLESSNESS BEFORE GOD

Earlier in this chapter, we mentioned God's people wandering the wilderness in Exodus and Numbers. Psalms 106:9–11 outlined the root of their wickedness in relation to God's grace to them. The psalmist states the following:

> We have sinned like our fathers,
> We have committed iniquity, we have behaved wickedly.
> *Our fathers in Egypt did not understand Your wonders;*
> *They did not remember Your abundant kindnesses,*
> *But rebelled* by the sea, at the Red Sea.
> *Nevertheless He saved them for the sake of His name,*
> That He might make His power known.
> Thus He rebuked the Red Sea and it dried up,
> And He led them through the deeps, as through the wilderness.
> (my emphases)

God's people were shown to be unfaithful because they were forgetful of his faithfulness. Yet despite their lack of memory of or meditation on his works, God delivered them for the sake of his name, per verse 8 of Psalms 106. God's name is tied to his people, and God does all things for his glory. The implication and application of this is serious for us. If you are reading this and profess to be a Christian, than you are claiming to have been redeemed by God through his greatest work in history, the crucifixion of his Son, wherein he bore our sin and endured in full the wrath of God for God's people. This is something we are commanded to remember and reflect on. Just hours before he went to the cross, the LORD Jesus instituted with his disciples the LORD's Supper, commanding them to take the bread and drink the cup to remember his body given and blood shed for the remission of sins in the new covenant (Luke 22:7–14; Matt 26:26–30). We are to be people who are continually reflecting on God's works, revealed in Scripture and culminating in his greatest work, which is the cross of the LORD Jesus Christ. This work was validated by the resurrection of the

LORD Jesus on the third day. We are to remember his faithfulness and his love. We are to remember all that he provides. In Psalms 103:1–5, David states the following:

> Bless the LORD, O my soul,
> And all that is within me, bless His holy name.
> Bless the LORD, O my soul,
> And *forget none of His benefits*;
> Who pardons all your iniquities,
> Who heals all your diseases;
> Who redeems your life from the pit,
> Who crowns you with lovingkindness and compassion;
> Who satisfies your years with good things,
> So that your youth is renewed like the eagle. (my emphases)

David calls us to bless the LORD, and at the end of verse 2 reminds his audience to forget none of God's benefits. He proceeds to list them. The benefits David list are centered around sinners being forgiven by God, restored to a relationship with God, crowned with God's faithful unending love, and satisfied with all he provides. Throughout Scripture, we as God's forgetful people are called to remember his benefits, his works, and his faithful love, especially if in the present we face the darkness of despair and depression. Despair and trials are common to man. David knew trials well, but he held fast to the works of God for strength in the present. Upon hearing Goliath defy the armies of the Living God and seeing his fellow Hebrews shrink in fear, David volunteered to fight Goliath. His source of strength was revealed earlier in 1 Samuel 17:37, when God had given the lion and the bear into his hands to destroy as he protected his sheep. He knew that God would deliver, based on God's past providential care in his own life. We are called to remember that God reigns, even when all seems lost, as it did for the Jews and Mordecai in the opening chapters of the book of Esther.

ADONIRAM JUDSON'S DESPAIR

The greatest missionary that ever came from the United States (at least, in my humble opinion) was a man named Adoniram Judson. Born August 9, 1788, he went on to spend his life in Burma for the fame of the LORD Jesus. In 1840, he translated the Bible into the Burmese language.[1] What is not often readily known about Judson is that, after having lost his daughter and hearing of the death of his father back home in the states, he went into a great depression. He had lost wives and children, and the darkness of loss seemed too much, too consuming for his weary soul to bear. He gave away every penny he had. He wrote to Brown University and returned the doctorate degree they had given him. He returned any honors commended to him. He withdrew to the edge of the jungle and dug a grave, where he would sit and meditate on the meaning of death. As time went by, Adorinam gradually recovered a testimony of God's faithful love, in even the darkest moments of life.[2] He faced his dark hour, but he never faced it alone, though he felt the emptiness of loss. God is faithful to his people and his love everlasting. In those types of moments, it is those truths we need to remember. We need to remember the Savior who despaired in the garden, anticipating the cup of God's everlasting wrath that he would drink in full; yet, he also submitted perfectly to the Father's will. We need to remember the love of God the Father for his people, a love that did not spare his only Son, but put the LORD Jesus on the cross and crushed him for our iniquities so that we could experience God's smile instead of his everlasting displeasure. We need to remember God's works in Scripture. We need to remember stories like those told in Esther, where all was bleak and dark. It did not make sense, but resulted in a deliverance that no man could have planned or performed. Believer in the LORD Jesus, remember all God's benefits! He is the same today, yesterday, and forevermore (Heb 13:8; James 1:17). God is faithful. God is good. God reigns.

1. Federer, *Great Quotations*, "Adoniram Judson."
2. Federer, *Great Quotations*, "Adoniram Judson."

STOP WORRYING, GOD REIGNS

"The sky is falling" seems to be the battle cry of the western evangelical church! All is going wrong! Politically, we are losing this or that. While there are some concerning trends, we see repeatedly in the book of Esther, as well as in all of Scripture, that God reigns. He providentially rules over all things and brings everything under the sun to its decreed end. In the Sermon on the Mount, Jesus taught his disciples,

> Do not worry then, saying, "What will we eat?" or "What will we drink?" or "What will we wear for clothing?" For the Gentiles eagerly seek all these things; for your heavenly Father knows that you need all these things. But seek first His kingdom and His righteousness, and all these things will be added to you. So do not worry about tomorrow; for tomorrow will care for itself. Each day has enough trouble of its own.

Jesus calls us to forsake our anxiety over what we will eat, drink, wear, who wins the election, what laws may be passed, or what diagnosis we may get. We are called to an active faith in an active God who reigns over all things in history, even the details of our everyday lives. We are called to focus on the LORD Jesus' kingdom and his righteousness. During trials, loss, and even the possibility of poverty, how can God's people do that? How can God's people do this considering all the liberalism or the perceived moral decline of western society? The answer of the book of Esther is to stop worrying, for the one true God reigns over all. Remember God's works in Scripture, culminating in the cross. Reflect on what God's works in Esther communicate about his power, providence, and purposes. Trust the unwavering and unending love of God for his people. Be bold in truth, fixing your eyes on living for and proclaiming the kingdom of Christ Jesus. No matter what comes your way, may God's providential care for his people lead you to live life by the motto "stop worrying, he reigns."

DISCUSSION QUESTIONS:

1. Why does the book of Esther conclude with an extensive call to celebrate Purim and remember what God has done for the Jews?

2. List out all the benefits that Jesus brings his people. How do those benefits affect your everyday life?

3. List out all your anxieties and troubles. What does the truth of God's providential care mean for each worry and trouble you are facing?

4. Considering our world's social climate, how does the narrative of Esther compel you to deeper rest in Christ, along with greater boldness in following him?

Bibliography

Baldwin, Joyce G. "Esther." In *New Bible Commentary: 21st Century Edition*, edited by D. A. Carson et al., 442–52. 4th ed. Downers Grove: InterVarsity, 1994. Logos Bible Software.

Barker, Kenneth L., and John R. Kohlenberger III. *Expositor's Bible Commentary: Abridged Edition*. Vol. 1, *The Old Testament*. Grand Rapids: Zondervan. 1994. Logos Bible Software.

Cross, F. L., and E. A. Livingstone, eds. *The Oxford Dictionary of the Christian Church*. 3rd rev. ed. Oxford: Oxford University Press, 2005.

Federer, William J. *Great Quotations: A Collection of Passages, Phrases, and Quotations Influencing Early and Modern World History Referenced according to their Sources in Literature, Memoirs, Letters, Governmental Documents, Speeches, Charters, Court Decisions and Constitutions*. St. Louis: AmeriSearch, 2001. Logos Bible Software.

Martin, J. A. "Esther." In *The Bible Knowledge Commentary: An Exposition of the Scriptures*, edited by John F. Walvoord and Roy B. Zuck, 701–13. Wheaton: Victor, 1985. Logos Bible Software.

Smith, James E. *The Minor Prophets*. Joplin: College Press, 1994.

Tomasino, Anthony. "Esther." In *Zondervan Illustrated Bible Backgrounds Commentary, Vol. 3: 1 & 2 Kings, 1 & 2 Chronicles, Ezra, Nehemiah, Esther*, edited by John Walton, 468–505. Grand Rapids: Zondervan, 2009. Logos Bible Software.